# IT'S BOUQUET – NOT BUCKET

# IT'S BOUQUET – NOT BUCKET

Harold Snoad

Book Guild Publishing
Sussex, England

First published in Great Britain in 2009 by
The Book Guild Ltd
Pavilion View
19 New Road
Brighton, BN1 1UF

Second Printing 2010

Third Printing 2010

Fourth Printing 2010

Typesetting in Garamond by
Keyboard Services, Luton, Bedfordshire

Printed and bound in Great Britain by
CPI Antony Rowe

A catalogue record for this book is available from
The British Library

ISBN 978 1 84624 351 6

# Contents

# *Preface*

My intention in writing this book is not only to provide the millions of fans of *Keeping Up Appearances* with a 'companion' to the series in which I tell you about the making of the various episodes – how things were achieved, amusing moments that you never got to see, etc. – but also to give you some interesting information.

In the course of reading it, I suspect that you will become quite intrigued by some of the events that occurred over the six years the series was being made. These 'events' were problems that I certainly never experienced with any of the other very successful shows I was responsible for during my twenty-eight years of producing and directing comedy series for the BBC. However, I can assure you that everything I have written here is one hundred per cent true!

Please bear in mind that Hyacinth would expect you to be properly attired reading this and have a suitably superior bookmark to hand if you are interrupted by someone thoughtlessly telephoning you at such an inconvenient time!

Hope you enjoy it.

# How It All Started

The situation comedy series *Keeping Up Appearances* is extremely popular in both the UK and in many other countries (sixty-six at the last count). It is particularly loved in the States where – in common with *Are You Being Served?* (the second series of which I also directed) – it has become almost cult viewing. In fact, according to the programme buyer for Public Broadcasting at the Comedy Central Channel, its their most popular show ever.

There were five series – totalling forty episodes – plus four 'specials' made for transmission at Christmas. I was both the producer and the director of the series. In general terms the producer checks that the scripts are up to the expected standard and looks after the financial and contractual side of things, whilst it is the director's job to coordinate and supervise every aspect of the programme as eventually seen by the viewer. This entails directing the actors in their performances including suitable 'business' (i.e. what they are seen to be doing at any particular moment) and, all in all, obtaining the very best interpretation of the script. The director is also responsible for 'directing' the cameras so that they are offering the right shot at the right moment enabling the action (the story) to be shown to the viewer in the best possible way.

At the time I read the script for the pilot episode of *Keeping Up Appearances* I was working on the sixth and final series of another project of mine – a very popular situation comedy called *Don't Wait Up* which starred Tony Britton and Nigel Havers as father and son doctors, 'Toby' and 'Tom Latimer'. In television – for some extraordinary reason! – we are contractually only allowed to work the artists on

1

six out of seven days in the week and, because this was the cast's day off, I was in my office at Television Centre instead of rehearsing.

Having spent the morning with my PA dealing with a mass of internal BBC memos and dictating replies to fan letters regarding *Don't Wait Up*, I decided to buy a sandwich and have this in my office whilst reading the script that had just been sent me by the then Head of the Comedy Department, Robin Nash.

As I started to munch through my sandwich, I turned the pages of the script and I immediately became hooked by the character of 'Mrs Bouquet' – her adventures, her very high opinion of herself and the way she felt she was being let down by her relatives 'on the other side of town'. The script was written by a comedy writer called Roy Clarke who had been responsible for several shows over the years – the best known, popular and longest running being *Last of the Summer Wine*.

By the time I had reached the final page I had decided that this was a great idea. I could already see the comedic potential and I knew that the viewers would love to watch the day-to-day adventures of a snob – particularly when things didn't go well for her and she would suffer as a result of her own actions. I immediately decided that I would definitely like to be part of the project by being the show's producer/director. I informed Robin Nash of my interest and he then told me that whilst it hadn't been written with anyone particular in mind for the role of Hyacinth he thought that the actress Julie Walters might be very suitable.

I went away and considered this suggestion very carefully but I was not entirely sure that Robin was right. Julie was, and still is, an excellent actress but, somehow, I thought that Hyacinth needed a 'stately galleon' – not only in physical size and bearing but in vocal terms. I felt that, in this instance, Julie Walters would not be right for the part.

There is an excellent casting directory called *Spotlight*. Having been in the business for many years, I was well aware of the vast majority of the 'bigger' names contained within its pages (i.e. those most likely to be considered for the leading role in a series). However, no human being could possibly immediately call to mind every thespian on offer and, like other producers and directors, I regularly used the volumes (four for actors and four for actresses) as a 'mind jogger'. I sat down that afternoon and started to search through the pages for likely contenders – in my opinion – for the role of Hyacinth.

By the time I had keen through the A–D, E–K and L–P volumes of 'Actresses' I had jotted down a few names, but I was not totally confident that they were really right for the part. As I was ploughing through the Q–Z volume I turned over a page and was greeted by a picture of Patricia Routledge. Immediately I knew that I had found the answer – she would be wonderful in the role.

I telephoned her agent (a lady called Patricia Marmont) and explained the situation. She said that her client might well be interested and asked me to send a copy of the script round to Patricia Routledge's home. This I did and the next day the agent rang me to say that her client had read the script and was, indeed, very interested and wanted to meet up with me and discuss it further – perhaps over lunch.

I explained that I was busy rehearsing *Don't Wait Up* – so would Patricia Routledge like to come over to the rehearsal block and have lunch with me the following day in the canteen there? Not the most elegant of venues but a practical suggestion in the circumstances. Later that afternoon the arrangement was confirmed.

The following morning I explained to my cast during rehearsals that I wouldn't be able to have lunch with them that day as was normally the case because I was having a meeting with Patricia Routledge, who I was considering offering the leading role in a new comedy.

Some of the cast looked a little uneasy and one of them jokingly asked me if I knew what I was doing! He wasn't referring to her talents as an actress but to the fact that she had a reputation within show business for sometimes being a bit of a 'dragon'. At the time I wasn't aware of this but I decided to put on my fireproof suit, check my insurance, and adopt an optimistic attitude.

Patricia Routledge duly arrived and we had an amicable lunch and discussed the script. She was slightly concerned that the programme would be recorded in front of a studio audience – but she was one of many artistes who are uneasy about such a prospect until they become familiar with the process and appreciate the advantages of having a live audience – not only for the actors but also the viewers at home. When you watch comedy in a theatre or a cinema you are with other people and laughter is infectious. However, at home there could well be just a couple of you watching or you may even be alone and the genuine reaction of a studio audience (not a laughter track!) can really enhance the viewers' enjoyment.

Towards the end of our meal the cast of *Don't Wait Up* got together and played a huge joke on me as they passed our table on their way back to the rehearsal room. Tony Britton – who, by his own admission, did not always arrive at rehearsals dead on time – stopped and knelt down in front of me and asked whether I would be kind enough to allow him another forty-eight hours to complete the five hundred lines I had given him for being late the previous morning!

Tony moved on and was replaced by Nigel Havers and Dinah Sheridan (she was playing Tony's wife – Nigel's mother) who begged forgiveness for chatting during rehearsals. Simon Williams (who played Nigel's NHS partner) apologised for mucking up one of his lines that morning. One by one the whole cast generally 'bowed and scraped'. As the last member moved on Patricia turned to me and said, 'They obviously adore you!'

Whilst it may sound immodest, that, in a way, was true. Over the twenty-eight years I directed programmes I got on extremely well with the various casts and the writers. They respected me because they recognised that, with my many years of experience, I knew what was I doing. When it comes to making a comedy programme, this means knowing how lines should be delivered to get the best out of them, understanding comic timing (essential!), having a good feel for the 'business' that you suggest to the artist concerned and, in general, having a developed sense of comedy and a visual imagination as to how things should best be depicted on the screen.

All the various members of my many casts over the years – people like Ronnie Barker, Leslie Philips, Dick Emery, June Whitfield, Martin Jarvis, Diane Keen, Richard Briers, Tony Britton, Nigel Havers, Dinah Sheridan, Francis Matthews, Geraldine McEwan, Marti Caine, Susan Hampshire, and so on – enjoyed our working together and we have remained friends long after the various series finished.

That weekend we completed the last episode of the sixth and final series of *Don't Wait Up* and had a wonderful end-of-series party at Television Centre. The cast, George Layton who wrote the series, and myself (plus my wife, Jean, and the various partners of other members of the cast) then went round to an extra farewell function laid on by Nigel Havers. After six very happy years of working together the final parting was tearful – sadly, a little different from a certain element of the party held at the end of the last series of *Keeping Up Appearances* – but more about that later.

The casting of any show is of paramount importance. Whilst there is no way that a cast, however brilliant, can make something which is patently obviously unfunny funny, a good strong cast, experienced in playing comedy is essential. It also helps enormously if they get on well together and work as a team – without any airs and graces about their own talent. It is also vitally important that the actors realise that when they go into a studio to record an episode in front of an audience it is a rather different ball game to what they might have been used to. It is not like the theatre where the experience of playing the same piece night after night – although all audiences are slightly different – can give them confirmation of where the laughs are, the timing of same, and how they and the director could perhaps do something in a slightly different way to achieve a laugh that doesn't always seem forthcoming. Even in the old days of weekly rep the cast generally had eight bites of the cherry but in the recording of an episode of a television situation comedy your first night is also your last night. The next day you move on to a new episode.

I thought about the cast for *Keeping Up Appearances* very carefully. Clive Swift (with whom I had worked before on a series called *The Further Adventures of Lucky Jim*) seemed to be an excellent contender for the part of Hyacinth's long-suffering husband, Richard. I asked him to come in and see me and, although the part in the first episode was pretty small, he could obviously see the possible potential and said that he would like to be involved.

The next character I wanted to cast was Elizabeth, Hyacinth's next-door neighbour, and I immediately thought of Josephine Tewson. Since I had first worked with her twenty years earlier on a Ronnie Barker series called *His Lordship Entertains* I had cast her in a lot of different shows because she is quite brilliant in this sort of role and her comedy timing is second to none. Because I knew her so well I didn't, initially, even go via her agent. I just rang her at home, said I had this part available and asked her whether she would be interested. She immediately said 'yes, please' and we never looked back. As usual she was superb and a perfect foil for Hyacinth.

I had worked with Judy Cornwell some years previously (on a Dick Emery Christmas show) and I thought that she would make a wonderful Daisy – not that I'm suggesting that she is anything like her in real life! Although I had met Geoffrey Hughes socially we hadn't worked together, but it seemed quite a funny idea to have two matching characters, shall we say, slightly 'larger than life'. Again Geoffrey is far from being an idle slob when he's not playing Onslow. In the first series the part of Rose was played by Shirley Stelfox.

Whilst on the subject of casting, this seems an appropriate moment to mention the other members of Hyacinth's family. Obviously if you are a fan of *Keeping Up Appearances* (and if you're reading this book you probably are) you will be aware of them anyway but, at least, it will remind you. Her other sister, Violet, lives in a fairly expensive property with her husband, Bruce, who has made a lot of money from being a bookmaker. During the series it becomes obvious that the marriage is on a distinctly rocky basis – largely due to his rather odd habits.

Hyacinth's father lives with Daisy and Onslow. His habits of going missing for one reason or another, his interest in ladies or re-enacting his memories of serving in the army during the war are often the basis of problems for Hyacinth and the rest of the family although, more often than not, we tend to hear about the trouble he is causing rather than actually see him in action.

Finally, there is Hyacinth and Richard's son, Sheridan, who is away at college. Although he is often on the phone to Hyacinth (usually asking for money for some new – and often rather bizarre – interest) he is never seen during the series. Hyacinth is very proud of him and admires his keenness to get involved in new things but Richard – who is having to come up with the money being asked for – is not as enamoured and is fed-up with making the requested payments. He can also see why Sheridan might be taking up these new interests – although Hyacinth seems quite oblivious to this.

Whilst all the casting contracts were being drawn up I was considering where we might film the location elements – in particular (assuming the pilot episode was deemed a success) the ones that were obviously going to be regular locations – Hyacinth's home plus Onslow and Daisy's on the 'other side of town'.

From experience I knew that it would be sensible to start with the one likely to be the trickiest. In this case we were talking about Onslow and Daisy's home, which needed to be set in a fairly 'down to earth' area. When you succeed in finding this sort of location it's always quite tricky explaining to the owners why you would like to film there. If it's a more upmarket property it's a lot easier. You can comment on the beautiful landscaped lawn, the leaded-light windows, the fountain on the lovely rockery and the Georgian pillars by the front door. It's not quite the same telling the owner of an Onslow type property that you want to film there because you love the garage door hanging off its hinges, the rusty motorcycle parts alongside the cracked concrete path and the gasometer overlooking the back garden!

Unfortunately this sort of venue can also present problems – from which most productions have suffered over the years. Although you may make all the right overtures to the owner of a suitable property, agree on a facility fee for filming outside their house (normally, and especially in the case of a situation comedy, it is just the exterior – the interior will be a set built in the studio), when you come to do the actual filming you can have problems. As well as needing eyes out of the back of your head to ensure that items of equipment, props and so on don't go 'walkies', you can also find yourself being 'blackmailed' regarding noise. In other words, having obtained the necessary silence required to film a shot, as soon as you call 'action' someone a few yards down the road just happens to, coincidentally, open a window and turn on some music – sometimes in the form of a ghetto blaster. When the perpetrator is asked if they would be kind enough to turn it off the reply is 'Yeah, of course – for fifty quid'. Or, they'll drive past you several times on their motorbikes – unless you pay them not to do so. In short, working in certain areas can be quite a pain in the proverbials as well as for the show's budget, and can considerably slow down the filming process!

In case you are wondering why a certain degree of noise is any problem – after all the viewer would expect some areas to be noisy – let me explain. It is essential that, at the time of filming, you have the area as quiet as possible. The reason is that a location scene is made up of a number of shots taken separately and then joined (edited) together afterwards. If the area isn't quiet when you film the various shots the background sound (cars starting and stopping, people chatting, dogs barking, children playing, etc.) will 'jump' every time the shots are edited together. For example the sound of a car passing will suddenly cut out when the shot changes to another one filmed where there was no car passing at the time.

Care has to be taken, therefore, to ensure that sequences are filmed with as little background noise as possible. After the shots have been edited together to form the sequence in question a dubbing session is held and a background track (called a 'buzz track') of noise applicable to the circumstances and type of location area is then added at a suitable level.

At this stage perhaps I should explain that I had decided some years ago that, if a project requires quite a lot of location filming, it was not a good idea to do this in London. Every day each member of the cast would have to come from their own homes to either a central point – perhaps Television Centre in West London – before moving on to the location or sometimes direct to the actual location for make-up and to be costumed before the start of filming.

Likewise, the members of the crew (camera, sound, lights, design, props, make-up, costume) and the production team (the director, his or her production manager, production assistant and the assistant floor manager) would all have to travel from *their* respective homes to the location – which, for some people, could be right the other side of London. This journey could quite easily take up two hours of their agreed twelve-hour day and a further two hours going back again at night. In other words only eight hours of the twelve are spent filming. Apart from that, the noise level (traffic, aircraft) and the general 'busy-busy' of a capital can lose you a lot of time and often mean a huge number of retakes.

I proved that it was considerably easier to find a suitable area out of London, negotiate a good deal at a hotel to accommodate the unit and work from there. That way we could be on location half an hour after leaving the hotel with the knowledge that it would only take twenty minutes or so to get back there again after filming. Although the hotel accommodation had to be paid for, it still worked out considerably cheaper. In short, you're filming for eleven hours a day – not eight – and the members of the unit aren't worn out and frustrated as they would be travelling backwards and forwards across London. Overall, doing things this way, filming that would have taken six weeks in or around London could be achieved in a month somewhere else – which also, of course, meant that I was saving the BBC money because I was employing the artistes and crew for a shorter period. An extra bonus was the fact that, as they are staying away together, everyone gets to know each other socially, which strengthens the 'team spirit'.

When looking for a suitable location for Daisy and Onslow's home I did some preliminary research and, for various reasons, narrowed it down to a couple of possible areas – one in Leicester and the other in Coventry. With my production manager for this pilot episode (Murray Peterson) I set off to visit the two council estates in question.

We duly arrived at Leicester and tracked down the first one. I parked the car and was in the process of getting out when a middle-aged man passed us and said, 'I wouldn't leave it there, mate – a couple of minutes and you'll have no wheels!' Although we initially laughed at this remark, we decided to make some enquiries. After a chat with the local police, we discovered that he wasn't joking.

We therefore dismissed this option and drove down to Coventry. Touring around a council estate on the outskirts of the town we passed a small street (Mitchell Close), which I immediately thought would he ideal. It was only about fifty yards long with about a dozen or so houses. On the left-hand side there was one house which, from the outside, seemed perfect for Daisy and Onslow's home. Although there was a space in front of the property which, because of its position, could be described as the 'garden', it was, in fact, merely a bare patch of hard uneven earth – 'soil' would be too kind a description. I immediately recognised this as having the potential we needed. Fans of the series will remember that Onslow had an old banger dumped in front of the house. That was, of course, added by our props department along with various other bits of rubbish but we could hardly have put the old banger on top of a reasonable piece of front lawn or a decent bed of flowers. By the time we had added our own broken gate and an upturned oil drum to disguise the concrete post that held up the real fence – which we removed when we were filming – we were pretty well there. We also temporarily swapped their front door for our own (in a pretty tatty state and with a Sellotaped cracked pane in the glass) so that we could take it back with us to the studio in London as a direct match when we needed to see the inside of the door for interior scenes in the hall.

The road was a cul-de-sac and behind the fence at the end there was a breakers yard with piles of old cars in evidence. As the road was very narrow – two cars couldn't pass – I decided to make use of the turning circle at the end of the road by having 'Richard' always park his car there, which meant that he was parking with the breakers yard in the background. This was ideal and went a long way to helping with the way Hyacinth looked down her nose at the area. Having come to an arrangement with the breakers yard that they would not smash up cars whilst we were actually filming we were home and dry.

Jackie, the wife of the council tenant in the house I needed, was very helpful and agreed to my suggested fee for filming and the other people in the road were also very obliging. Normally I wouldn't have consulted all the neighbours, but as it was such a small 'community' it seemed the right thing to do.

Obviously, when a unit is filming somewhere, there is inevitably some degree of inconvenience not only to the residents of the actual property but also to their neighbours. We have a number of lamps running off a generator truck (which has to be parked round the corner out of camera shot and where it won't be heard working away), camera equipment including tracks (a set of rails on which the camera dolly travels when the camera has to follow moving action), sound equipment, and the props needed for the sequence being filmed, plus the attendance of the cast and the various members of the unit – a total, in the case of *Keeping Up Appearances*, of about thirty people.

There are also certain practical problems. We can stop filming for a few moments whilst someone is creating noise when driving to and from their home, but what is far more difficult is what is called 'continuity'. For instance, we could be halfway through filming a sequence in which we have established a certain vehicle in the background when it is removed by the owner in order to go to work or down to the shops. Certainly not unreasonable behaviour on their part – it's their car outside their house and they obviously have every right to move it – but from our point of view we have seen the car in some shots of a particular sequence and then suddenly it's not there in other shots in the same sequence, which means that, when we edit the various shots together, it looks as if Paul Daniels has used his influence or, for American readers of this book, David Copperfield!

The way to get round this is for the production manager to have a tactful word – before we start filming – with owners of any vehicles likely to be seen in the background of a sequence to establish whether they will be using their car. If they are planning to go out later they are asked if they would be kind enough to move it now so that it won't disappear in the middle of the sequence. The reverse applies, of course, to cars returning halfway through a scene. Sometimes they are politely asked if they would mind parking round the corner for the time being.

There is, as I mentioned earlier, inevitably a degree of inconvenience involved, but filming has to take place somewhere – otherwise there would be a lot less to watch on television – and, on the whole, people are very helpful and are only too happy to oblige. Also, of course, they are rather pleased to know that they – and their friends – will be able to watch the programme and see their home on the telly!

Normally, on these occasions, it is customary to only pay a fee to the occupiers of the actual house we are using – otherwise you could finish up paying people half a mile away! In the case of Onslow's road, however, we were obviously going to be 'taking over' the area, so I decided that I would talk to the other residents and suggest that we paid a fee of two hundred pounds to a charity or local 'good cause' of their choice – perhaps towards a computer for a school or a TV for an old folks' home, thereby encouraging a community feel. They appointed one of the residents to represent them and she came back to us a few days later to say that they had given the matter a lot of thought and had come to a decision – they were going to split the cheque between them! In fairness, they did apportion it according to people's needs.

Next we set about finding Hyacinth's home, which, for practical reasons, ideally didn't want to be too far away from Onslow's. We asked an estate agent for suggestions for suitable areas to start looking and off we went. Roy Clarke, the writer – who as I was to later discover is not the most practical person – had described Hyacinth and Elizabeth talking to each other from their respective front doors which, as they were living in detached houses, could easily be as much as forty feet apart. In which case it would have been more like shouting to each other than talking! I had this problem very much in mind when we were looking for suitable properties.

As we were slowly driving down Heather Road in the Binley Woods area (on the outskirts of Coventry and, surprisingly, only about a couple of miles away from the location I had chosen for Onslow and Daisy's), I suddenly spotted two properties which I considered would be ideal. One was a bungalow – which I could easily imagine being tarted up with hanging baskets, shutters, bushes in tubs by the front door and so on – and alongside it a house which had its front door on the side. Ideal! We immediately made contact with the two owners who agreed to assist.

One of the many jobs the director has to do is to come up with some suitable opening and closing titles for a series – a task which I had been successfully carrying out for more than twenty years. Up until just before this time the visual content of these had always been accompanied by a catchy tune. However, there had now started to be a vogue for title music with lyrics – *Only Fools and Horses* and *One Foot in the Grave* being perfect examples.

I decided that this would also be appropriate for *Keeping Up Appearances* and having contacted Nick Ingman who had composed signature tunes for me for some years, I asked him whether he had any ideas where I could find a suitable lyricist. He thought for a moment and then sensibly commented that by the time I had told the lyricist what I had in mind I might just as well write the lyrics myself. He was also aware that I had a reasonable track record for writing because I had co-adapted nearly seventy episodes of *Dad's*

*Army* for radio, written two other comedy series for that medium and a series for television.

Accepting that he had made a reasonable point, I put my thinking cap on and came up with some suitable and amusing lyrics to accompany the visuals I had planned for the opening and closing sequences. In the case of the opening titles these started with an establishing shot of the outside of Hyacinth's home when suddenly two small boys wander into picture eating crisps. One finishes his and drops the empty packet on the pavement right outside the bungalow as they continue on their way. We then see Hyacinth, who has obviously witnessed this, pull back her net curtains and look at the offending crisp packet in horror. She then appears at the front door and strides purposefully forward to retrieve the 'rubbish' – carefully ensuring that her skirt doesn't rise up as she bends down to pick up the packet! On the way back to the door she glances at the lawn and checks the height of the grass and then studies her front step because she thinks someone has trodden on it leaving a slight mark. At this point Richard arrives home and makes to give her a kiss on the cheek. With a horrified look around to see if the neighbours might have spotted his outrageous behaviour, she hastily pushes him inside and closes the front door.

Nick had composed a bright and catchy theme and the lyrics accompanying it were sung by a young actor called Rob Rawles (he subsequently played Hyacinth's milkman) who, at that time, had just finished a stint playing the lead in *Me and My Girl* in the West End. The lyrics (written, as I said, by myself) start as Hyacinth rushes out of her front door to retrieve the crisp packet and go like this:

From first thing in the morning
Till last thing at night
She's busy 'Keeping Up Appearances'.
Are her nets still white?
Is the grass upright?
Does her knocker shine?
[*Hyacinth looks down at her step and says 'Has somebody stood on my step?'*]
Yes, everything has to be right

[*Richard arrives and kisses her cheek.*]
And certain things kept out of sight.
[*She hurriedly pushes him indoors.*]
Oh, it's a full-time job
'Keeping Up Appearances'.
[*reprise*]
'Keeping Up Appearances'.

The closing sequence sees Hyacinth in the back garden bringing out a basket to take her washing in. As she keeps reaching under the length of the double sheet pegged out on the line it becomes obvious that her and Richard's underwear have been drying under it to avoid any possibility of these items being seen by the neighbours! The lyrics for the closing went like this:

From first thing in the morning
Till last thing at night
She's busy 'Keeping Up Appearances'.
Are the windows clean?
[*She glances up at them.*]
Can her slip be seen?
Is the compost tidy?
[*She looks down the garden, then looks at a nearby garden bed and says, 'Is that a pest on my rhubarb?'*]
There's no such thing as credit
Or running into debit.
[*this line spoken*] It's not an easy life 'Keeping Up Appearances'.
You have to keep your end up
In everything you do.
Library books go back on time
Though you're only halfway through,
And you only go to the doctor
If you've gone down with something nice.
Oh, it's a full-time job
'Keeping Up Appearances'.
[*reprise*]
'Keeping Up Appearances'.

Before we go on let me remind you of the storyline for Episode 1 and give you details of the cast:

## EPISODE 1

**Plot:** Hyacinth is busy preparing for one of her candlelight suppers when her sister, Daisy, rings to tell her that Daddy is in hospital having had an accident whilst engaged in his regular pursuit of chasing the ladies. As a result Hyacinth has to drop everything and go and visit Daddy, but on the way she calls in to see Daisy. Whilst there we see her register horror at the untidiness of Daisy's home and garden, the behaviour and general appearance of her sister's husband, Onslow, and the tartiness of her other sister, Rose. Hyacinth and Richard then go on to see Daddy.

Having got back from the hospital, Hyacinth has her neighbour Elizabeth in and over coffee tells her about Daddy's accident but not what he was doing at the time! The Major rings Hyacinth and when he asks her whether she would like some flowers for her function that evening she accepts and goes round to his home only to discover that he is in a particularly amorous mood!

In the course of the episode we see how Hyacinth deals with people like her postman and the man who comes to read her meter.

**Cast:** Hyacinth (*Patricia Routledge*); Richard (*Clive Swift*); Liz (*Josephine Tewson*); Daisy (*Judy Cornwell*); Onslow (*Geoffrey Hughes*); Rose (*Shirley Stelfox*); Doctor (*Bruce Alexander*); The Major (*Peter Cellier*); Postman (*Leo Dolan*); Meter Man (*Paul Toothill*); Mr Oxley (*James Ottaway*)

The location filming for the pilot episode went extremely well – we used the exteriors of Onslow and Daisy's and Hyacinth's whilst the exterior of a school in Leamington stood in for a hospital. I also, of course, filmed the shots I needed for the opening titles and the closing sequence. When we got back to London I had an editing session with my excellent VT editor Andy Quested. I should perhaps explain that scenes shot on location are still traditionally referred to as 'filming' sessions despite the fact that, nowadays, the scenes are generally shot using a video camera. When 'video' first came in, it was normally only used for sequences recorded in the studio – location sequences were still shot on film. However, the definition of the end results (particularly in terms of sharpness of the picture) was very different and when, for instance, there was continuity of someone arriving outside their home on location, opening their front door and stepping inside (shot on film), and then seen coming away from the front door into their lounge (in the studio and recorded on video), it was not ideal as the change of mediums was extremely obvious. Even when there was no direct continuity it still jarred to go from a scene shot on film to an interior recorded on video and vice versa. It was for this reason that myself and other directors began to use video cameras on location which means that the quality of the end results looks pretty well exactly the same and the joins are 'invisible'.

Now, where was I? Oh, yes, we then had a dubbing session to add the necessary sound effects – and the aforementioned 'buzz track'. Robin Nash popped into the dubbing suite during this session, took one look at Patricia Routledge's performance up there on the screen and admitted quite happily that I had been right – she made a perfect Hyacinth.

We then duly started rehearsals for the studio elements. We began by having a read-through of the scenes involved (as is normally the case) and then I set about blocking the action, which means giving the artistes the moves and business that I have worked out to go with their dialogue. Particularly in busy scenes (for example those in the kitchen) this can sometimes be quite complicated and it is essential that, once settled, the moves and whatever business the artistes are engaged in doing during the scene stay the same so that, when I come to work out my camera script three or four days later (i.e. how I propose to shoot the scene when we are in the studio), everything that happens is always done at exactly the same place within the dialogue. Consistency is extremely important.

In the rehearsal room the 'walls' of the various sets (i.e. the kitchen, hall, lounge, bedroom etc.) are marked out on the wooden floor by the assistant floor manager – working to the designer's plans – with narrow sticky tape (each set in a different colour) so that the artistes can relate to where they are in the various rooms. There are also doors on free-standing frames to assist with the timing of any entrances and exits called for during the action of a scene, plus, of course, basic items of furniture (generally *extremely* basic) to represent the real items the artistes will be using on the day of recording.

Rehearsals went very well and it was obvious that the members of the cast were appreciative of the fact that I – as the director of the show – had worked out in advance how the piece could best be played in terms of moves, business and general 'pace'. Over the years every director will come across the occasional actor or actress who, in a way, somehow resents the fact that the director has done his homework and worked out an overall 'plan of campaign'. These are the actors who like to start with a blank piece of paper and 'see what develops' without the director's input. This is a rather arty touch which encourages a sort of 'direction by committee' approach which can quite often cause problems and which, for practical reasons and lack of time, certainly doesn't work in television on a show with a weekly turn-round.

Clive Swift, who is an extremely good actor, was of this type and there were just a few occasions over the six years when he was slightly reluctant to accept a particular move or a piece of business without looking at it 'in depth'. However, on the whole, he generally finished up doing what I had suggested as well as coming up with some brilliant performances.

On the third day of the rehearsals for the pilot episode we had a visitor – Roy Clarke (our writer) – which, in itself, was quite a surprise. While it is customary for writers to attend the read-through, the technical run-through and the actual studio recording of many – if not all – of the episodes, Roy never did this on any of the series for which he was responsible. Apart from the basic practical problem – he lives in Yorkshire and seldom leaves that area (in fact, he is jokingly known as 'the Yorkshire Hermit') – it almost seems that he has never really shown that much interest in how an episode turns out. You rather get the impression that, once he has written the script and handed it over to the producer, his interest finishes. In fact, he actually admits this in the section given over to *Keeping Up Appearances* in an excellent American book called *Great Britcoms* written by Gregory Koseluk.

A few years later, Roy was to tell me (much to my amazement) that he never watched transmissions of other situation comedies – a strange admission because, surely, it's important to be aware of the 'competition' – and, even more surprising, he seldom watched his own!

Anyway, I introduced Roy to the members of the cast and he watched several scenes being rehearsed and expressed his pleasure at what he saw. He stayed and had lunch with us in the canteen at the rehearsal rooms, and it was during this meal that I described the opening titles and the closing sequence that I had planned and went over the lyrics with him. I didn't tell him that I had written them but there was nothing devious about this – it just never crossed my mind to do so. He listened to the lyrics with interest, smiled at the appropriate points and when I had finished commented 'sound's fine'. This remark – witnessed by Patricia Routledge and several other members of the cast – would be remembered a couple of weeks later.

The following evening I worked out my camera script – a lengthy process in which I had to decide exactly what shots I would need each of the six cameras to be giving me at every point during the recording of the studio elements of the episode in a couple of days' time. We were due in the studio on the Sunday and we had our technical run-through on the Friday. This takes place at the rehearsal rooms but is attended – hence the name – by the lighting and sound supervisors, the technical coordinator plus the designer (including his assistant and the properties buyer – 'props' ranging from items of furniture and pictures to absolutely anything which is needed in the course of the action) plus the costume and make-up designers.

The intention is to let them see the action, how the set is going to be used, where the director needs to position the various cameras, and allows everyone to become familiar with planned breaks involving a set change or a costume and make-up change. The run-through went very well (this is the first time the cast and the director actually hear the laughter of people watching the action and, although there are only half a dozen or so people, it is very rewarding). When we broke rehearsals later that afternoon I think everyone realised that we probably had a success on our hands.

On the Sunday in the studio the rehearsals went very well. This is, of course, the first time we have been on the proper set and with all the technical equipment – hence the reason these sessions are called 'camera rehearsals'. For those people unfamiliar with how it works each cameraman is given a list of the shots the director wants him/her to be offering at a particular point in the action. Each shot is numbered – there are generally about two to three hundred shots per half-hour episode, although this, of course, varies depending on how much of the episode is set 'on location' and, therefore, has already been pre-filmed.

The director sits in the production gallery watching a bank of TV monitors – each one being the output of one of the cameras. The vision mixer whose job is to cut from one camera to another at the point decreed by the director, sits on one side of him with their copy of the camera script and the PA on the other. The latter uses her copy of the camera script to read out the shot numbers so that the cameramen know which shot we are on at any given moment. She also calls out which camera the vision mixer will be coming to next – as a warning to that cameraman. For example, 'Shot 179 – 4 next' means that we are currently looking at Shot 179 and we will be coming to Camera 4 (he being responsible for presenting Shot 180 as planned by the director with the details given him in his shot list typed out by the PA) next.

During camera rehearsals the cameramen and soundmen hear the director on headphones (aka 'cans') as does the production manager, part of whose job it is cue the artists to start a scene or cue a character to make an entrance at the precise moment required by the director. In other words, he relays the director's instructions. During the rehearsals he also passes on any messages from the director (perhaps an actor is masking another character in a particular shot because he is leaning too far forward, for instance) and also ensures that scene changes are carried out swiftly and efficiently.

Alongside the production gallery is the lighting gallery, from where all the lights are operated, and the sound gallery, where the sound supervisor makes sure that the microphones being used on the studio floor are picking up everything they are supposed to and at the right levels. Also in the sound gallery is the sound operator who is responsible for playing in any music, sound effects, telephone rings and so on.

Essentially, everyone works to the director in order to achieve the end result he envisaged when he was working out his camera script. The programme is recorded in front of a studio audience (of about three hundred and twenty people) and it is their laughter that you hear when you watch the show at home. They are also shown the pre-recorded location sequences – in the correct order as the story evolves. Before we start recording the audience are made welcome by a 'warm-up' man. People who have never attended a recording of a show sometimes wonder why this is necessary; they say that it doesn't happen in the theatre, which is quite true. The difference is that in the theatre the 'action' only stops during the interval.

In television – because of required scenery and costume changes plus the movement of technical equipment – there are a number of breaks and the warm-up man is needed to put the audience at their ease and fill in during the gaps and also at any point when it is necessary to retake a section again for some reason. I used the services of one of the best warm-up men in the business, a chap called Bobby Bragg.

The recording of the pilot episode went extremely well and the following day, having watched a VHS of the recorded material and made my notes for the editing session (deciding where retakes should be used and also where small 'tightens', or cuts, need to be made between shots which will 'tighten' the action), I had an editing session with Andy and we finished up with a very strong episode.

In fact, just one look at the finished episode made the 'powers that be' immediately decide that it would be a very good idea to make a series.

I sent a VHS copy of the finished version of the pilot episode to Roy Clarke to show him how it had turned out. Two days later the telephone rang and it was Roy. Before saying anything else about the programme (which he subsequently went on to say that he had enjoyed) he attacked the opening titles and the closing credits in quite a vitriolic fashion. In fact, his opening remark was 'I hate the titles'!

Somewhat taken aback I politely pointed out that they were exactly as I had described them to him over lunch on the day he had dropped in at rehearsals. He went on to say that he didn't like the lyrics and I reminded him that I had gone over those with him at that same lunch. His reply to this was: 'At that time I didn't realise they'd been written.' I didn't think it was wise to pursue this comment any further, but it was a little difficult to understand how I could have gone over the lyrics with him if they *hadn't* been written?

I wondered whether the reason he was saying that he didn't like them was possibly because, as part of the closing credits, I had not only credited the singer but, in a small type size, I had given myself a credit as writer of the lyrics as is the perfectly normal practice. (I had not, however, paid myself anything for taking on this task.) He rang off, saying that he would think of an idea himself and come back to me.

Only recently I was talking to a colleague who has also worked with Roy Clarke who said that Roy had told him that one of the lines of my lyrics had said 'Do her knockers shine?' – an amusing but incorrect observation! (For those readers who are not aware of the double meaning of the word 'knockers', it is British slang for 'boobs' or, in perfect 'Hyacinth' English, 'breasts'.)

Three weeks later I still hadn't heard from Roy. However, in the interim, I had looked at the opening and closing sequences of other shows written by him and noted that they all started over an extension of the opening or closing situation – normally in a location setting. I wrote to him tactfully pointing out that whilst this worked well in projects set in idyllic countryside – *Last of the Summer Wine*, for instance, is filmed in the Yorkshire Dales – it wasn't quite as easy or picturesque with something set in a suburban street. However, I said that I was quite happy to commission another piece of music and go along the same lines as his previous projects if that was what he really wanted.

A further three weeks later I still hadn't heard from him. Unfortunately, I had also only received the script for Episode 2, although, at the time he had been contracted to write a further five episodes, he had promised that I would have received Episodes 2, 3 and 4 by then. When I returned after a week's pre-planned holiday I was pleased to see there was at last a letter from him with his suggestion for the title sequence. Previously he had told me that he would also let me know why he hadn't liked my version but there wasn't any reference to this.

Roy's idea was that at the beginning of each episode we would see Hyacinth playing the piano and singing a different number from *The Sound of Music* with cutaways to the other characters in the series expressing their opinion about her lack of talent as a singer through their facial reactions. His suggestion for the closing credit sequence was that we saw Hyacinth playing and singing 'You'll Never Walk Alone' – once again with reactions from the others.

I was somewhat perplexed with these ideas because the series was quite obviously more about a snob with illusions of grandeur than a woman who plays the piano and thinks that she can sing. Patricia Routledge's reaction was exactly the same as mine. She sent me a note saying that the idea left her speechless and that the series wasn't about inadequate artistic endeavour – that was only a very small part of it.

The scripts for Episodes 3 and 4 had also turned up whilst I had been away and I read these with interest. They now called for the occasional appearance of 'the Vicar' and I remembered meeting an actor called Jeremy Gittins at some general auditions I had held a few months previously. The fact that he didn't look like the usual stereotypical Vicar but was rather good-looking was immediately seized upon by our writer and the attempts by Rose to meet up with him became a running gag.

Eventually, it was agreed that the 'titles' project would be handed over to an outside firm who came up with the idea you see when you watch the show. I then directed this new sequence and Roy appeared to be happy with it.

As I said earlier it is part of the job of the producer of a series to consider the script content very carefully and, if he feels it is necessary, express any doubts he might have about certain elements by contacting the writer(s). They then discuss it amicably and come to an agreement. Inevitably a writer can, on occasions, become too 'close' to his own work and over the years I have always found that even the most successful and well-known comedy writers find it very useful indeed to have the thoughts and observations of a very experienced producer/director.

The ones that I have worked with over the years and with which I have had very amicable relationships include David Croft and Jimmy Perry, Jeremy Lloyd, Ray Galton and Alan Simpson, Ian Davidson, John Warren and John Singer, Dick Clements and Ian Le Frenais, Keith Waterhouse and Willis Hall, Hugh Leonard, Ronnie Barker (as Jonathan Cobbold), N.F. Simpson, John Esmond and Bob Larbey, Richard Waring, George Layton, among others. A pretty impressive list!

What is wrong with a script is not necessarily some major element – it may be just a series of smaller things – but, taken together, it can mean that the script may not be working quite as well as it should. A similar situation to divorce where the problem may be a string of little things and not necessarily that one party may have leapt into bed with someone else! I had already written to Roy making some tactful observations about elements of Episodes 2 to 4 but I hadn't had any response, and because Episodes 3 and 4 had arrived very late it was fairly obvious that 5 and 6 were also likely to be delayed. As time was marching on it was therefore going to be very difficult to get them into a reasonably finished state to enable copies to be sent out to the members of the cast before the start of the location filming for the five episodes which, along with the original pilot, would constitute the first series.

Eventually, the missing two scripts turned up and my new production manager (David Lardner) and myself were able to go back to the Coventry area to look for the new locations required for the five episodes. Whilst there, we made contact with the owners of the house we had used for the exterior of Onslow and Daisy's and the bungalow we used for the exterior of Hyacinth's to tell them that the pilot episode had been deemed a great success by the powers-that-be. We went on to say, as we had originally told them, that this meant that we would need to use their homes not only to film further location elements for this batch but also, possibly, for subsequent series in the future. To my horror when we talked to the owners of the bungalow this piece of information didn't seem to go down too well!

What I hadn't been told originally was that when we had spoken to Rosemary – she and her husband, Tony, owned the property – he hadn't been at all keen and really didn't want to know, although, at the time, she had told us that everything was fine. Basically, he was now saying that he didn't want us to film there, which would mean that, because we had already established their bungalow as Hyacinth's home in the pilot episode, we would have to find another location and reshoot all the scenes again. This would also have affected the interiors we had shot in the studio because, to a degree, the layout of those sets had, of course, been based on the property we were using for the exterior. Fortunately, I managed to persuade him to change his mind and as he became more familiar with the process of location filming he accepted it far more readily.

As I still hadn't received any response from our writer about the various doubts I had raised regarding Episodes 2 to 4 it was becoming increasingly obvious that it was unlikely that I stood much chance of getting anywhere with my reactions to Episodes 5 and 6. Because time wasn't on my side, I therefore reluctantly decided that I had no alternative but to make various alterations here and there myself to all five episodes and the scripts were then sent out to the members of the cast.

Let's have a look at the five storylines used for the other episodes which comprised the first series and, when relevant, I'll give you background details about the making of that particular episode. I'll also tell you about any additional locations we used – although I won't give you the precise house number of a private residence because that is a little unfair to the owners. If, however, you are a keen enough fan of the series to want to go and look for the exact property you should be able to find it. Incidentally, in the short descriptions of the content of the various episodes throughout this book I tend to concentrate more on Hyacinth's adventures because, whilst what is going on at Onslow's, for example, is certainly very funny, on the whole it is easier for you to recognise an episode from what happens to Hyacinth.


## EPISODE 2

**Plot:** Hyacinth has invited the new Vicar and his wife to tea. She has also invited Elizabeth, who is terrified that she might break one of Hyacinth's Royal Doulton cups. Just before the Vicar is expected to arrive Hyacinth is horrified when Daisy and Onslow turn up in their tatty old car to tell her that Daddy has run off with a gypsy. She manages to get rid them by sending Richard off with them and the Vicar and his wife duly arrive. Unfortunately, just as she is pouring out the tea Daisy and Onslow return because Onslow doesn't have enough money for petrol and Richard has forgotten his wallet. Hyacinth is then even more shattered when Rose arrives heavily wrapped up in an emotional crisis. Rose is delighted to learn that Hyacinth's Vicar is there and wants to discuss her problems with him – especially when she sees that he's young and good-looking. It's not a very good day as far as Hyacinth is concerned!

**Cast:** Hyacinth (*Patricia Routledge*); Richard (*Clive Swift*); Liz (*Josephine Tewson*); Daisy (*Judy Cornwell*); Onslow (*Geoffrey Hughes*); Rose (*Shirley Stelfox*); Vicar (*Jeremy Gittins*); Vicar's Wife (*Marion Barron*); Gypsy (*Eileen Davies*); Passer-by (*Jill O'Hare*)

## EPISODE 3

**Plot:** Hyacinth and Richard are driving to a stately home that she is keen to visit when she suddenly decides that she ought to call in at Daisy's and check that Daddy is all right. Whilst they are there a woman arrives accusing Rose of having had an affair with her husband. Having established that Daddy is all right Hyacinth and Richard go on their way again. At the stately home she goes out of her way, much to Richard's embarrassment, to give other visitors the impression that she knows His Lordship well. She is then horrified to see Onslow, Daisy and Rose turn up – they are there because they think Richard deserves to be rescued from Hyacinth – and she dashes around hiding from them. Whilst crouching in a trench in the grounds they meet up with His Lordship although, at the time, Hyacinth thinks he's one of the gardeners.

**Cast:** Hyacinth (*Patricia Routledge*); Richard (*Clive Swift*); Rose (*Josephine Tewson*); Daisy (*Judy Cornwell*); Onslow (*Geoffrey Hughes*); Rose (*Shirley Stelfox*); Angry Woman (*Liz Gebhardt*); Car Park Attendant (*Eric Carte*); Stately Home Visitors (*Les Clack, Stella Kemball*); His Lordship (*Michael Bilton*)

**Additional locations:** Petrol Station (Fina Service Station on the A423 at Princethorpe); int./ext. Stately Home (Broughton Castle, Banbury)

In this episode, as well as making any alterations I felt were necessary, I also came up with my first idea – of many – for getting more out of a situation. Namely, when Hyacinth and Richard are on their way to visit the country home and she changes her mind and tells Richard to turn the car round because she feels she should be visiting Daddy. Having done so, she then changes her mind again. This was supposed to happen three times within a fifty-yard stretch of road. Whilst I could have merely had Richard find a side turning to assist with this manoeuvre I decided to use a petrol station forecourt and build up on the proprietor's annoyance as he naturally assumed they were going to buy some petrol only to find that they repeatedly went past the pumps, out the other end and back onto the road.

This was the first time we saw Onslow's dog bark at Hyacinth from the wrecked car in their 'garden', causing Hyacinth to finish up in the hedge. Incidentally, there was an amusing moment whilst we were filming outside Onslow's. He and Richard are in the garden talking when a woman drives up and dashes past the two of them in order to have a row with Rose inside. I established her arrival by seeing her car pull up and then having the camera follow her over to Onslow and Richard before she dashes inside, leaving the audience looking at the two men who then continue their conversation. Unfortunately, she hadn't applied the handbrake properly and the car started to run backwards down the road. Geoffrey noticed this out of the corner of his eye and although he tried not to let it affect him he suddenly stopped in mid speech, burst into hysterical laughter and said, 'I'm sorry, Harold, I tried to keep going.' The car finished up in a hedge thirty yards down the road!

# EPISODE 4

**Plot:** Hyacinth checks that Richard is suitably attired before letting him leave for work and then reminds Elizabeth that today is the day they have volunteered their services in the charity shop. They are about to leave when Hyacinth receives a call from Daisy telling her that there is a lady in Daddy's bedroom saying that he has asked her to marry him. Hyacinth decides she ought to call into Daisy's on the way to the shop. Unfortunately, she forgets that they will be going in Elizabeth's car and suddenly realises, to her horror, that this will mean that Elizabeth will see where Daisy and Onslow live! Hyacinth goes to elaborate lengths to avoid this by getting Elizabeth to stop outside a very pleasant house in a smart street and saying that is where Daisy lives. She then climbs over their rear garden wall and runs to Daisy's real home. When she gets back to the car twenty minutes later they drive on to the charity shop to join up with the eminent Mrs Councillor Nugent. To Hyacinth's horror, Rose turns up and donates some of her clothes which, as Mrs Nugent is not pleased to discover, turn out to be flimsy articles of underwear totally inappropriate to a charity shop.

**Cast:** Hyacinth (*Patricia Routledge*); Richard (*Clive Swift*); Liz (*Josephine Tewson*); Daisy (*Judy Cornwell*); Onslow (*Geoffrey Hughes*); Rose (*Shirley Stelfox*); Daddy's Fiancée (*Gretchen Franklin*); Councillor Nugent (*Charmian May*); Mr Duxbury (*Norman Lovett*); His Mate (*Denis Bond*); Postman (*Leo Dolan*)

**Additional locations:** Ext. charity shop (11 Regent Grove, Leamington); ext. smart house which Hyacinth leads Elizabeth to believe is Daisy's (Northumberland Rd, Leamington); part of garden with wall Hyacinth climbs over (Cloister Crofts, Leamington)

This is the first time we meet Councillor Mrs Nugent – a character who turns up in several episodes. Because my production manager and I couldn't find a suitably posh house that also had exactly what we wanted in terms of the rear garden wall which Hyacinth climbs over, we had to split the action between two locations. The

27

scenes outside the front of the house and when Hyacinth first appears in the rear garden (plus the owners watching her) were filmed at one location and the element of her climbing over the wall at another.

An amusing moment occurred when the actress playing Mrs Councillor Nugent arrived outside Onslow's to return Rose's clothes. When she rattled the letterbox to get their attention the whole thing came off in her hands.

All actors are capable of making mistakes in their dialogue (known as 'fluffs') and sometimes this can result in them – and their fellow artistes – being unable to keep a straight face and starting to laugh (known as 'corpsing'). During a scene on the landing outside Daddy's bedroom, Geoffrey Hughes had to respond to a remark made by Daisy by saying, 'It's remarks like that that help to cool the first flush of happy marriage.' It's not the easiest of lines to say and he got it slightly wrong, and as a result he and Pat just couldn't stop laughing – three times over. It was fine on the fourth take!

## EPISODE 5

**Plot:** This is the first time we see Hyacinth's milkman. Hyacinth has volunteered her services along with Richard's and Elizabeth's to assist at a charity luncheon at the church hall. Meanwhile, Daisy – who is worried that Onslow is no longer attracted to her – has decided to try and make him jealous by getting a seventeen-year-old motorcyclist friend of Rose's to appear to be taking an interest in her. At the church hall it is pretty obvious that none of the other volunteers can stand Hyacinth as they try and hide whenever they see her approaching. Daisy has got Onslow to go to the church hall by telling him that Richard wants to see him, but the real reason becomes obvious when during an exterior community hymn-singing session in which Richard and Onslow find themselves involved, Daisy turns up as the pillion passenger of the good-looking motorcyclist. However, Hyacinth is far more worried to see Onslow and Daisy there than Onslow is on seeing Daisy with the motorcyclist!

**Cast:** Hyacinth (*Patricia Routledge*); Richard (*Clive Swift*); Liz (*Josephine Tewson*); Daisy (*Judy Cornwell*); Onslow (*Geoffrey Hughes*); Rose (*Shirley Stelfox*); Vicar (*Jeremy Gittins*); Milkman (*Robert Rawles*); Mrs East (*Jeanne Mockford*); Mrs Dobson (*Tricia Thorns*); Neighbour (*Ian Burford*); Youth (*Jonny Lee Miller*); Ladies at church hall (*Linda James, Pamela Abbott*)

**Additional locations:** Ext. of church hall (Christchurch, Northampton)

This was the first time we had needed the exterior of the church hall (the interior was going to be a studio set) and my production manager and myself went to look for a suitable location around the Leamington area (where we always stayed) and Coventry – where, of course, we already had the locations for Hyacinth's and Daisy's homes. There were certainly a number of halls but we couldn't find one that had a large area of space outside – which we needed – or, indeed, one that 'shouted' church hall because it was very obviously adjacent to a church. Also any possibilities that we did find tended to be very noisy because they were alongside particularly busy main roads.

As it happened, because of a large annual event in the area, our unit hotel on the outskirts of Leamington wasn't going to be able to accommodate us for certain days of our filming period so we looked at a map with a view to trying somewhere further afield and possibly killing two birds with one stone – putting ourselves somewhere else for the church hall scenes, with a hotel in that same area for the days they couldn't take us in Leamington. We decided to try Northampton, where we almost immediately found just what I wanted – a large hall right next to the church, plenty of space outside for the filming and, looking ahead, a good-sized interior with a stage if we ever needed to film inside for certain episodes (as, indeed, it subsequently turned out that we did). It worked very well and, from then on, all the church hall material was filmed there.

Although, of course, I was always giving the cast 'business' – part of the director's job, as I've said – I was rather pleased with the action I gave Hyacinth in this episode of picking up each glass that the Vicar had just put down on a tray having dried it, drying it again and putting it down on another tray. There was an unintentional amusing moment in the scene where Onslow and Richard go to a pub together for a beer. As Onslow took his first drink from his glass it obviously went down the wrong way and he gulped, started laughing and said, 'Can we start again, Harold?'

## EPISODE 6

**Plot:** Hyacinth and Richard are due to attend the christening of their niece's baby. On the way to the church (not their local one as used in Episode 5) they call in at Daisy's in order to pick up Rose to whom they are giving a lift to the church because Onslow's car will be full with himself, Daisy, Daddy and his girlfriend. Whilst at Onslow's, Hyacinth is, as usual, appalled by the state of the place and their idea of a celebratory drink. When they arrive at the church the Vicar and the guests wait for a very long time and there is still no sign of the niece and her baby. Finally the Vicar receives a call saying that they have broken down in the countryside a couple of miles out of town. Anxious to get away from the Onslow crowd, Hyacinth says she and Richard will go and collect them. However, they have great difficulty finding them until they realise that they were the gipsies in a broken-down old van that they had passed a few minutes earlier! Richard manages to charge their battery from his car, but then he and Hyacinth have to turn up at the church as passengers in the dilapidated vehicle because their own battery has become flat as a result. A highly embarrassed Hyacinth emerges from the van extremely upset at being associated with such people.

**Cast:** Hyacinth (*Patricia Routledge*); Richard (*Clive Swift*); Liz (*Josephine Tewson*); Daisy (*Judy Cornwell*); Onslow (*Geoffrey Hughes*); Rose (*Shirley Stelfox*); Vicar (*Gerald Sim*); Reg (*Bruce Bennett*); Dennis (*Jonathan Fryer*); Mrs Midgely (*Patricia Leach*); Hippies (*Rick Friend, Richard Aston*); Stephanie (*Laura Shavin*)

**Additional locations:** Ext. of church for christening (St Mary's, Northampton)

The location work for the five episodes went very well as did the studio recordings. By the way, one of the things that presented a little bit of a problem was what Onslow was watching on his telly. In the pilot episode I used an extract from a Western feature film but, to use it, the BBC had to pay, quite reasonably, a fee. At that stage, of course, I had no idea just how often future scripts would call for Onslow to be seen watching TV. As soon as it became obvious that it would be virtually every episode I realised that this could become a very costly operation.

I therefore decided that it would be much cheaper for the BBC if we made 'films' of our own. During every filming period you have to schedule a certain amount of time (usually a couple of days every three weeks) as 'standby' to allow for shooting sequences that weren't able to be filmed as originally planned because of inclement weather. If an element of these two days hadn't been used because the weather hadn't been all that bad – or we had managed to pick up the lost sequence on another day because something hadn't taken quite as long to film as myself and my production manager had originally thought – there were occasions when we could see that we would probably have the odd afternoon free.

In case you are wondering why, in these instances, we didn't just move on to another sequence, this isn't always possible because it quite often involves artists who aren't contracted to join us until later and locations and vehicles that are not available to us earlier than the originally arranged date. For various reasons, therefore, there generally came a time in most filming periods when we could see that on a certain day we would have a few spare hours. I used these to make the 'movies' you saw on Onslow's telly – or to be more precise, the 'extracts' you saw.

The first one was made in some woods alongside the unit hotel and was a spoof horror movie which featured a girl being chased by a phantom-type character. It only ran for about three minutes and starred our very pretty make-up girl. Everyone joined in the making and Geoffrey Hughes had a go with the sound boom, although he lost the job fairly quickly because he managed to get the microphone in shot so much!

The sequences were edited together by Andy, my VT editor, and appropriate mood music was added. Andy called the first one *Virgin's End* and from then on gave each one a title that continued the 'End' theme.

I eventually made *Gangster's End* (in the breakers yard near Onslow's), *Hostage's End* (in a disused and about-to-be-pulled-down element of our location hotel), *German's End* (on a railway siding) and *Pilot's End* (in a barn). When any dialogue was involved I wrote it but I generally tried not to have too much of this because, when played on the telly at Onslow's, dialogue from the set would have intruded into the main action – especially at the high sound level that Onslow was supposed to watch television.

I therefore hit a happy compromise that the visuals seen on his TV should mainly be accompanied by mood music and effects. There were also occasions when we used horse racing, which made a change and was much cheaper than real movies. Eventually there were so many occasions when Onslow had his telly on that the various sequences were used quite a number of times – although I tried to avoid having the same sequences in consecutively transmitted episodes.

Although I used members of my team in *Virgin's End* I used professional actors and stuntmen in all the others. Even having to pay them a fee, it was still a huge saving over the cost of the copyright fees that would have to have been paid every time I used extracts from real movies.

There was one occasion in Series 5 when we played a joke on Geoffrey during the dress run-through. When he thumped the telly he found himself watching some slightly, shall we say, 'dubious' material. His reaction during the playing of the scene was wonderful as he strove to keep a straight face and remember his lines! When we finished the scene he looked straight into camera and jokingly said, 'You bastards!' Judy and Mary said they hadn't understood the sequence!

Incidentally, as Judy Cornwell reminded me recently, there was an occasion during the studio recording of one of the episodes in this first series which required Onslow and Daisy to suddenly sit up in their bed together as a result of which – and, presumably, because there was a fair amount of weight involved in this operation – the legs of the bed collapsed throwing the two of them downwards and backwards into the scenery. It didn't take that long to sort this out and it should have been fairly easy to go back and pick up the action a couple of speeches earlier, but every time we started again the two of them burst into hysterical laughter. From then on their bed was given extra support!

After the recording of the final episode of this batch, we had an 'end of series' party. This was something I had done for many years and, more recently, on such series as *Ever Decreasing Circles* and *Don't Wait Up*. The cast and everyone involved in the making of the series get together in a function room with a few bottles of wine, some soft drinks and some 'nibbles' and enjoy themselves. Obviously this has to be paid for and I had usually thrown twenty pounds into the kitty and asked the writer and the regular members of the cast to chip in a fiver. When I put this to the cast a few days earlier everyone agreed – although, for some reason, Patricia didn't seem to be too keen on the idea. There was no point in asking Roy Clarke for a contribution because he wouldn't be attending the recording and, in fact, was never present at any of the forty-four episodes we eventually made.

Another thing I always did at 'end of series' parties was to get my editor to put together a tape of 'out-takes' – that is, things that had gone wrong during the shooting of the series – generally actors' dialogue errors or completely forgotten lines and, sometimes, problems with props. This was shown at the party to everyone's great enjoyment.

In fairness and in contradiction to what I have just said, Patricia was both thoughtful and generous. Once, shortly after the first series when my wife and I were dining at a restaurant near Patricia's home to celebrate our wedding anniversary, we were presented with a plant she had delivered earlier. The other occasion was Christmas that first year when she sent me a case of champagne. This, however, was at a time when she was 'learning' a lot from me – by her own admission – about the often quite tricky world of situation comedy. However, those two events were really the only examples of her generosity that I can remember.

On the strength of the viewers' reaction to the first series and their obvious love of Patricia in the role of Hyacinth a second series was commissioned. Incidentally, our writer had made absolutely no comment about the alterations I had made to the scripts but then, as I touched on earlier, perhaps he was unaware of them because he hadn't watched the shows!

# The Second Series

This time it was going to be ten episodes, which, in itself, was quite a compliment to the show's success. Normally, at that time, a sitcom series consisted of either six or seven episodes. Apart from this being the usual number transmitted in the UK, it meant that the total of two successive series was thirteen – the number of episodes that interested America and other countries apparently because it coincided with there being thirteen weeks in a quarter.

Location filming dates and studio recording dates were arrived at and Roy Clarke was contracted and given plenty of notice as to when the scripts should start arriving. Needless to say until the producer/director has a script in his possession he has absolutely nothing to go on. He has no idea what other locations are required; he can't tell his designer what additional studio sets will be needed; he can't begin to think about casting actors required to play additional characters – in short, there is very little he can start to sort out until he is in possession of the scripts.

Shirley Stelfox wasn't available when we came to make the second series so I had to think again. I suddenly remembered Mary Millar (who hadn't been available when I was originally casting because she was in *Phantom of the Opera*) and asked her to come in and see me. She did so wearing a miniskirt she had bought especially for the occasion. She was obviously rather embarrassed wearing it but told me much later that she thought it might increase her chances of proving that she would make a good Rose. Whilst I am certainly not adverse to seeing an attractive lady wearing a mini skirt it wasn't for that reason that I gave her the part! Mary's track record was well known and as soon as we'd read a scene together I had no doubts that she would be perfect. She was also a delightful 'warm' lady to have around, although I'm not saying that Shirley wasn't!

'Emmet' (Elizabeth's brother) was only introduced at the time of the second series and I chose David Griffin because I had been most impressed with his work in the comedy series *Hi-de-Hi!*

Robin Nash suggested that it might be useful if a gentleman called Christopher Bond (at that time a script reader/editor at the BBC but previously a successful writer of scripts himself) were to act as an intermediary between myself and Roy Clarke. He wasn't going to re-write anything – and I had no intention of doing so either unless I was put in a position of having to – but was there to discuss with me any doubts that I had and, if he thought they had substance (and it turned out that 99 per cent of the time he totally agreed with my observations), to put them to Roy Clarke – I never discovered why but Roy obviously didn't seem to like it when I approached him.

Four months earlier a deadline of between the middle and end of February had been agreed for me to receive all ten scripts. On 20 January I received the first two! Incidentally, you probably imagine that scripts for a television series just turn up and the director shoots them. Not on this series! Anyway, Christopher and I read through these two scripts together (reading alternative characters) and, while we thought there was some very funny dialogue, we still had a string of little points that we weren't totally happy about – though, thankfully, only a few major ones.

## EPISODE 1

**Plot:** This episode revolved around the arrival of a strange man who is obviously staying next door with Elizabeth. When Hyacinth first sees him he is in the process of putting out a milk bottle and appears to be wearing just a towel round him. Hyacinth immediately jumps to all the wrong conclusions and is horrified that Elizabeth is letting the area down by having a liaison with some strange man! It isn't until later that she learns that he is, in fact, Elizabeth's brother, Emmet, who is staying with her after his marriage had fallen apart. Hyacinth is particularly enthusiastic about his presence next door when she learns that he is musically inclined to the extent of putting on productions with amateur dramatic societies. She immediately sets out to impress him with her own vocal talents – which is quite a task!

**Cast:** Hyacinth (*Patricia Routledge*); Richard (*Clive Swift*); Liz (*Josephine Tewson*); Daisy (*Judy Cornwell*); Onslow (*Geoffrey Hughes*); Rose (*Mary Millar*); Emmet (*David Griffin*); Milkman (*Robert Rawles*)

## EPISODE 2

**Plot:** The elderly Mrs Fortescue telephones and asks Hyacinth whether she happens to be going into town and if she and Richard could give her a lift. Hyacinth regards Mrs Fortescue as very eminent and immediately agrees to assist – although Richard is none too keen. Having called and picked her up they are driving into town when Richard happens to spot Daisy and Rose waiting for a bus and, much to Hyacinth's horror, stops and also gives them a lift. She is even more appalled when the three ladies who are squashed in the back of their car seem to be getting on so well – to the extent that, when Daisy spots a pub up ahead, she suggests they all pop in for a drink. Hyacinth decides to wait outside in the pub's car park and having discovered that Onslow also happens to be in the pub sends Richard in to get them out as quickly as possible. However, time passes and they still haven't emerged. Hyacinth decides to have a look inside through one of the pub's windows but this backfires on her and her social standing is in danger of being dealt quite a blow.

**Cast:** Hyacinth (*Patricia Routledge*); Richard (*Clive Swift*); Liz (*Josephine Tewson*); Daisy (*Judy Cornwell*); Onslow (*Geoffrey Hughes*); Rose (*Mary Millar*); Emmet (*David Griffin*); Mrs Fortescue (*Jean Anderson*); Pub Customer (*Leonard Lowe*); Neighbour (*Michael Burrell*)

**Additional locations:** Ext. Mrs Fortescue's (house in Northumberland Terrace); ext. of pub (The Rugby Tavern, Rugby Road, New Cubbington)

It was with this episode that I had one of the major problems that I mentioned earlier. The original script called for Hyacinth to send Richard in to try and get them out of the pub as quickly as possible before Daisy and Rose let the side down too much. Because of the presence of Onslow's bike outside the pub – they had seen him riding it earlier – she realises to her horror that he is also inside. Hyacinth doesn't want to go in herself – presumably on the basis that visiting a public house would do nothing for her image, especially as she would be seen with Daisy, Rose and Onslow!

Mind you, it could well have been argued that if Hyacinth was so desperate to keep in with Mrs Fortescue – who obviously felt that it was perfectly all right to go into a pub – surely Hyacinth would have gone in there as well? Anyway, Hyacinth decides to wait outside in the car. So far so good. After a supposed time lapse of about twenty minutes, or so the original script said, she gets fed up waiting and, just as she is on the way to the pub door to see if she can catch a glimpse of the four of them inside – if Onslow was with them it would be five – she suddenly sees two ladies that she knows coming along the pavement. Rather than be seen outside a pub she looks round for somewhere to hide and chose to do this by climbing up onto the back of a lorry parked in the pub's car park. The writer's intention was that whilst she was up there the driver would come out of the pub and drive off with her still on board.

As far as I was concerned there were several things about this section that didn't ring true and wouldn't work. For a start, I can remember thinking, wait a minute, how are the audience supposed to know why Hyacinth is panicking on merely seeing two ladies approaching (it's not as if they were characters that the audience would recognise) who just might notice Hyacinth going into a pub – hardly a huge offence. Then, when Hyacinth wants to hide, why on earth would she climb up onto the back of a lorry? Anybody else finding themselves in a similar situation would merely duck down behind the lorry until the two ladies had passed by.

My answer to that is that our writer seemed, at times, to have a sort of 'cartoon' mind, in which he saw the final 'picture' of a sequence and then wrote things – sometimes with all logic totally thrown out of the window – so that events finished up to make that 'picture'.

During the five series there were quite a few examples of this. It would only be fair to acknowledge that this 'lack of logic' seems to work for another of Roy Clarke's series, *Last of the Summer Wine*, but I think the reason for this is because that is set in the Yorkshire Dales in a sort of time warp, and as the characters are not as 'real' as those in *Keeping Up Appearances*, this allows their adventures to be rather more bizarre.

Because I had been unable to discuss with Roy any doubts I had about previous episodes, Christopher and I both knew that, regrettably, there was very little chance of him accepting our reservations and agreeing to do a re-write – so I took it upon myself to adapt the script so that it still finished in the way that he had intended but the events leading up to that point made a lot more sense. I had a woman wearing an overall up a pair of steps cleaning the outside of the pub windows. During one of the earlier scenes in which Hyacinth is sitting in the car waiting for Mrs Fortescue and the others to come out I established that, as it is a warm, sunny day, the window cleaner is obviously feeling hot in her overall and we see her take it off and hang it on the back of the steps. We subsequently see her realise that she needed some clean water and take her bucket into the pub.

It was at this point that I had Hyacinth – fed up with waiting – decide to go and look inside. However, as she can't see through the lower part of the pub windows because they are coloured and made of frosted glass, she hits upon the idea of using the window cleaner's steps to discreetly look through the upper part of the window. Now, when the two ladies come along, she is definitely doing something infra dig. We see Hyacinth notice the ladies and hear her say to herself, 'Oh no, not Mrs Parker-Finch.' Now I had got the message over that she knows the ladies and, not unreasonably, is worried about them seeing her up a pair of steps looking through a pub window.

I had her panicking, then quickly donning the nylon overall, grabbing the chamois leather and assuming the role of the window cleaner. Thinking that they've moved on I then had her coming down the steps only to find the couple are still there admiring same plants in the pub's garden. Because Hyacinth needs something to do I then got her to move the steps towards the lorry and then, desperately in need of some further form of activity, use them to climb up onto the back of the lorry. When the two ladies appear to be looking in Hyacinth's direction, I then had her diving under a tarpaulin which is stretched across the floor of the vehicle. This was now a logical sequence because I had made some sort of sense of the extraordinary idea that she would hide from the two women by immediately climbing up on to the back of a lorry!

The window cleaner now re-emerges and retrieves the steps somewhat puzzled. The women move on and Hyacinth reappears from under the tarpaulin and is about to get down from the back of the vehicle – with difficulty because she no longer has the steps – when the lorry driver emerges from the pub and drives away with Hyacinth still on board. In short, I had achieved precisely what Roy had intended but with a lot more logic and fun. Patricia, who wasn't at all happy with the original, thought my version worked extremely well.

In the past, on all the various series I had produced and directed, I had never needed to show any member of the cast the writer's original script for any episode of a series. Once I had discussed any doubts that I had with the writer, the original was typed up – including any agreed amendments arrived at during our discussion – and copies sent out to the cast two weeks before the start of filming as is customary. Sadly, in the case of *Keeping Up Appearances*, I had no real alternative but to adopt a different approach. Patricia Routledge was undoubtedly the star of the series and – like me – wanted the end result to be as good as possible. There was no point in me (and Christopher) having reservations but doing nothing about them, having the script typed up, copies run off and sent out, and then finding, at that late stage, that Patricia, understandably, also wasn't happy with it.

Patricia generally held exactly the same views as us on what 'didn't quite work' or 'might work better this way' and, having read the original scripts (I sent her photocopies), she and I used to ring each other and talk about our doubts because, in the light of our experience of script problems with the first series, we – and Christopher Bond – knew that there was, unfortunately, very little point in going back to the writer and expecting him to consider our various reservations. The only option left was for me to make any alterations to the original script that we felt were necessary. Another very relevant factor was that if Roy was so far behind with the writing of this batch of ten episodes he was hardly likely to be in a position – or even possibly the right frame of mind – to consider doing any re-writes. As time moved on I realised that, unlike other well known writers that I had worked with, he very seldom seemed prepared to accept that a re-write might be necessary or even to consider the reasons why it was being suggested.

## EPISODE 3

**Plot:** Hyacinth has arranged another of her candlelight suppers but it is ruined when most of the people she has invited manage to find an excuse for not turning up. Although Rose hasn't been invited she arrives and starts to flirt with Emmet. If this isn't bad enough, Hyacinth is even more appalled when two of Rose's boyfriends also turn up and start having an intense row outside Hyacinth's front door as to which of them means the most to Rose. Much to everyone's horror Hyacinth has to resort to playing the piano and singing to drown out the noise. Given the choice, Emmet would have much preferred to have listened to the row!

**Cast:** Hyacinth (*Patricia Routledge*); Richard (*Clive Swift*); Liz (*Josephine Tewson*); Daisy (*Judy Cornwell*); Onslow (*Geoffrey Hughes*); Rose (*Mary Millar*); Emmet (*David Griffin*); Boris (*Dicken Ashworth*); Mr Helliwell (*Gregory Cox*); Man with Dog (*Stuart Sherwin*)

Incidentally, although Patricia needed to sing very badly in this series, in reality she has an extremely good singing voice and has appeared in a number of musicals. However, she is not that talented when it comes to playing the piano – especially when she has to 'act' singing badly at the same time – so in the scenes where she was required to play, the piano she used was 'muted' so that the keys produced no sound and she merely went through the motions of playing. In reality, a very talented gentleman called Chuck Mallett – who had worked alongside Patricia in the musical world and also used to play piano for Pat when she had her own cabaret show – played another piano off-screen.

The same thing applied to David Griffin who was totally non-musical. Again his renderings were sometimes played by Chuck or by Ray Moore (an MD from the musical theatre) and, on one occasion, Clive Swift helped out. Clive can play the piano extremely well and was often found enjoying himself doing so when the rest of us returned to rehearsals after a lunch break.

## EPISODE 4

**Plot:** Hyacinth and Richard go to a hotel for a golfing weekend at the invitation of the Major who Hyacinth thinks they ought to keep in with 'socially', especially as golf is very much an 'upmarket' activity. Apart from annoying the hotel staff and other guests Hyacinth foolishly accepts an offer from the Major to go for a drive in the country – whilst Richard is busy practising his golf – only to discover that the Major is still romantically interested in her! Rose is at the hotel having a fling with her latest boyfriend and when Onslow and Daisy arrive to pick her up they are privy to the sight of a bedraggled Hyacinth returning from running away from the Major in the countryside.

**Cast:** Hyacinth (*Patricia Routledge*); Richard (*Clive Swift*); Liz (*Josephine Tewson*); Daisy (*Judy Cornwell*); Onslow (*Geoffrey Hughes*); Rose (*Mary Millar*); Emmet (*David Griffin*); Major (*Peter Cellier*); Hotel Guests (*Dinah Sheridan, Bernard Archard*); Receptionist (*Sally Hughes*); Porters (*Christopher Mitchell, Eamonn Clarke*); Chambermaid (*Sharon White*)

**Additional locations:** For the exterior elements of scenes set at the hotel I used the front and the garden of the Chesford Grange Hotel on the outskirts of Leamington, which was very convenient because, at that time, it was our unit hotel.

The reception area, corridors and bedroom we needed for this episode were built in the studio but we also required the use of a large lounge for Hyacinth to go round testing the various settees and armchairs, not only for comfort but to ensure that they had been dusted to her satisfaction. We didn't have enough space left in the studio for such a large set to be erected so I needed to film this element on location.

The Chesford Grange Hotel didn't have a lounge that would be suitable but, in the course of our location recce, my production manager and I called into the Regent Hotel in Leamington's main street. The lounge was perfect and they were happy to let us film there. In reality, I only did the material that involved Hyacinth wandering around checking the furniture – watched by two fascinated guests – on location. My designer at that time (Tim Gleeson) then reconstructed one wall of the lounge in the studio. This was used for the dialogue elements of the scenes when Hyacinth sat down and started to bore the couple rigid by talking about her husband's important job with the council – a great exaggeration – and by showing them photographs of Sheridan. We had taken the sofa and chairs we were going to use in the studio element with us to the hotel so the continuity was right. Even the most discerning viewer would be hard pressed to see where the studio element of the lounge took over from the real thing on location.

Incidentally, it was very nice for Dinah Sheridan and myself to work together again because, as I mentioned earlier, we had previously done so on six series of *Don't Wait Up*, the show I was doing before *Keeping Up Appearances*.

This was the first time I became familiar with the interior of the Regent Hotel. I subsequently went on to use it as the unit hotel for the location filming for Series 3 onwards. Having now received all the scripts I was a little worried that some of the ten episodes contained very large elements of déjà-vu from the first series. I am not talking about 'running gags' – which are one of the ingredients of situation comedy – I am talking about episode storylines being repetitive with very little new happening.

I brought this to Robin Nash's attention but he told me not to worry. In the event I was right to be concerned because this 'repetition' scenario was, unfortunately, going to become even more obvious in the future.

## EPISODE 5

**Plot:** Hyacinth interrupts Richard in the middle of an important meeting at work with a series of family crises ranging from Daddy's suspected elopement to news that her brother-in-law, Bruce, is sulking up a tree because Violet won't let him wear one of her party dresses! Onslow and Daisy get involved – Onslow is very annoyed because Daisy interrupts him in the betting shop to tell him about Daddy. A missionary wishes he'd never called at Hyacinth's – although Emmet finds it very amusing, especially as it was he who had sent him round to her after the missionary had called at Elizabeth's.

**Cast:** Hyacinth (*Patricia Routledge*); Richard (*Clive Swift*); Liz (*Josephine Tewson*); Daisy (*Judy Cornwell*); Onslow (*Geoffrey Hughes*); Rose (*Mary Millar*); Emmet (*David Griffin*); Registrar (*Helen Christie*); Committee Chairman (*Simon Merrick*); Committee Member (*Robert McBain*); Missionary (*Brendan O'Hea*); Daddy (*George Webb*)

**Additional locations used:** Registry Office (Guildhall Rd, Northampton); Violet's (Newbold Terrace East, Leamington Spa)

This episode called for Daddy to go through various antics such as being lifted in and out of cars and sliding over walls under the guise of 'being asleep'. I found this very unbelievable and suggested to Roy – via Christopher – that it might be an idea if Onslow says he gave Daddy one of his 'pills' before they came out and then for Daisy to reveal that she hadn't realised this and had given him one as well. Roy agreed that this would make Daddy's adventures rather more believable. By the way, it was us that named Violet's house 'The Paddocks' (because of Bruce's job as a turf accountant) and the statues and satellite dish were all props added by my designer.

## EPISODE 6

The idea of attending Onslow's birthday party fills Hyacinth with horror. Mind you, Onslow is none too thrilled at the prospect of her turning up either. However, Hyacinth changes her tune somewhat when she discovers that she and Richard are going to be picked up by Rose's latest boyfriend in his limousine – so much so that she organises a cocktail party at her place so that, if she times things correctly and shows her guests out after her own function at the appropriate moment, it should coincide with the limousine's arrival and they cannot fail to be aware of the sort of vehicle she travels in! Unfortunately, the limousine is not functioning properly on the day and the boyfriend has to use another of his vehicles – a hearse. Until then even Rose didn't know he was an undertaker.

**Cast:** Hyacinth (*Patricia Routledge*); Richard (*Clive Swift*); Liz (*Josephine Tewson*); Daisy (*Judy Cornwell*); Onslow (*Geoffrey Hughes*); Rose (*Mary Millar*); Emmet (*David Griffin*); Major (*Peter Cellier*); Vicar (*Jeremy Gittins*); His Wife (*Marion Barron*); Jeweller (*Anthony Dawes*); Committee Member (*Robert McBain*); Mr Maranopolous (*Ivan Santan*); Chairman of the Committee (*Simon Merrick*)

Having seen Rose turn up in the hearse, the horrified Hyacinth tells her to get the undertaker to go round the block whilst she gets rid of her guests. However, getting rid of them takes rather longer than she envisaged and they are still in the front garden when the hearse returns. The original version of the script merely called for Hyacinth to distract her guests whilst she frantically indicates to the driver that he should go round the block again – and that this should happen three times.

The problem with this scenario was that it was pretty obvious that, unless Hyacinth distracted her guests in some specific way, the chances of all six of them not noticing the hearse starting to pull up outside the bungalow were pretty slim. Unfortunately, there was no dialogue provided for this 'distraction'. The guests merely stood around in the garden chatting to each other and looking at the flower beds – which weren't that impressive anyway! I helped the situation by writing dialogue for Hyacinth so that on the first and third occasions the hearse passes she hurriedly encourages her guests to turn away from the road as she draws their attention to aspects of the design of her property ('By the way, have you noticed our new flashings? The lead came from a disused monastery just outside Toulouse' etc.). On the second occasion I changed things so that they *do* see the hearse but stand silently in respect as it passes, which, of course, was perfectly reasonable but wouldn't have worked on all three occasions!

These changes went a long way to making the situation that much more believable.

There was an amusing moment during the filming for this episode in the scene where Hyacinth is in a taxi and Richard is outside on the pavement and bends down to talk to her just before the taxi drives away. It was a rather windy day and when he was in the middle of saying, 'Do we have any cocktails?', his hat suddenly blew clean off his head and bowled down the street.


## EPISODE 7

**Plot:** Much to his horror Richard learns that he is shortly going to have to take early retirement from his job at the council offices. Hyacinth, however, is thrilled at the prospect because it means that the two of them will be able to spend more time together – the main reason why Richard is so worried! On the other side of town, Rose is thinking about giving up men for life and becoming a nun. Meanwhile, Hyacinth thrusts herself on poor Emmet at the church hall in an attempt to impress him with her singing.

**Cast:** Hyacinth (*Patricia Routledge*); Richard (*Clive Swift*); Liz (*Josephine Tewson*); Daisy (*Judy Cornwell*); Onslow (*Geoffrey Hughes*); Rose (*Mary Millar*); Emmet (*David Griffin*); Vicar (*Jeremy Gittins*); His Wife (*Marion Barron*); Mr Penworthy (*Nigel Williams*)

This was the first time I had needed to see the Vicarage and we used the exterior of a private house for this in Leamington and put up a sign saying 'St Mark's'. As it happens we subsequently discovered that the Vicar of the church we used at Northampton was quite enjoying having us film at his church hall and was more than happy to let us film outside his Vicarage – which was in front of the church hall – which we subsequently did in future episodes.

## EPISODE 8

**Plot:** Daisy, Onslow and Rose arrive on Hyacinth's doorstep – to her usual horror – to tell her that a large local department store is holding Daddy 'hostage' until a £235 bill is paid for toys that he had walked off with. Hyacinth rings Richard at work and asks him to meet her at the store. When she arrives there she bumps into the eminent Councillor Mrs Nugent and also has to contend with the sight of Bruce galloping down the street outside the store dressed as a jockey and riding a pantomime horse!

**Cast:** Hyacinth (*Patricia Routledge*); Richard (*Clive Swift*); Liz (*Josephine Tewson*); Daisy (*Judy Cornwell*); Onslow (*Geoffrey Hughes*); Rose (*Mary Millar*); Emmet (*David Griffin*); Councillor Nugent (*Charmian May*); Frank (*Robert McBain*); Insurance Salesman (*John Owens*); Store Official (*John Pennington*); His Assistant (*David Warwick*); Salesgirl (*Juliet Douglas*); Daddy (*George Webb*)

**Additional locations:** Int./ext. department store (Debenhams, Northampton)

An amusing moment occurred whilst we were on location filming outside Debenhams for this episode. There was a delay, owing to some cars parked outside, in being able to do a shot in which Onslow's car needed to pull up outside the store. It was a one-way traffic system and Judy and Geoff had to go round the block several times. When I was ready to film the shot my production manager called them on the walkie-talkie. We waited for them to turn up but there was no sign of the car. Judy later confessed to me that this was because they had found a temporary parking space to wait for a few minutes which happened to be right outside a home-made sweet shop. They had gone inside – leaving the walkie-talkie in the car – bought some very fattening confectionery, and were stuffing themselves with this whilst I was wondering where they had got to!


## EPISODE 9

**Plot:** Hyacinth is thrilled silly about the imminent delivery of her new three-piece suite which she deliberately ordered from a store that has a royal warrant. Her next task is to ensure that a particular 'snobby' neighbour doesn't miss the arrival of the van with its royal crest on the side. Unfortunately things don't go quite according to plan!

**Cast:** Hyacinth (*Patricia Routledge*); Richard (*Clive Swift*); Liz (*Josephine Tewson*); Daisy (*Judy Cornwell*); Onslow (*Geoffrey Hughes*); Rose (*Mary Millar*); Emmet (*David Griffin*); Van Driver (*Nick Burnell*); Driver's Mate (*David Keller*)

When Hyacinth was expecting her new three-piece suite the original script called for her to dash out of the front door with Richard following carrying two traffic cones, which she uses to reserve the area the furniture van will need for parking. My immediate reaction was why would Hyacinth of all people just conveniently happen to have official police cones in her house? The addition of Hyacinth's line 'We acquired them for just this sort of occasion' went a little way to help.

Because Hyacinth wants to ensure that a certain neighbour witnesses the arrival of the new suite, she plans to ring her at the appropriate moment, which will take the neighbour to her telephone which Hyacinth knows is near the neighbour's front window. When the van arrives Hyacinth needs time to make the call so she tells an embarrassed Richard to ask the driver to go round the block. Unfortunately, whilst the driver is doing this the van has an accident and her lovely new suite subsequently turns up outside Hyacinth's on an open-back lorry – which Onslow has borrowed to pick up the old suite that Hyacinth is giving them – that just happened to pass the broken-down delivery van.

Whilst I felt this relied rather heavily on a lot of coincidences, I was quite prepared to go along with this apart from one thing which was that, when the suite arrived on Onslow's lorry in the original version of the script, there was no sign of the delivery men – just Onslow, Daisy and Rose. Although we are talking comedy and not real life, it was difficult enough to accept that a reputable firm with a royal crest would sink to using the back of a tatty lorry to deliver an expensive suite, let alone that they would hand it over lock, stock and barrel to an unknown driver – especially when he looks like Onslow! In my version I at least had the delivery men arrive on Onslow's lorry with the suite.

Incidentally, in that episode we learned that Hyacinth was planning to give her old suite to Onslow and, indeed, in the next episode – the last one in the series – it was seen at Onslow's. However, when we came to make the third series I mentioned to Roy that I didn't think that it ought to still be there because its presence was undoubtedly out of keeping with the general 'downmarket' feel of their home. Roy agreed with me and wrote some extra lines establishing that Onslow had sold it because it constantly reminded him of Hyacinth – he also needed the money!

## EPISODE 10

**Plot:** Hyacinth decides that they ought to take Daddy out for a picnic. Unfortunately, when they call in at Daisy's to pick Daddy up, he decides to commandeer Richard's car. There is no alternative but to accept Onslow's suggestion that they give chase in his car. Hyacinth and Richard pile in with Onslow, Daisy and Rose and they follow Daddy. Richard is extremely worried about what is going to happen to his car but Hyacinth seems more concerned about the fate of her cut-glass condiment set which she packed as part of the picnic equipment.

**Cast:** Hyacinth (*Patricia Routledge*); Richard (*Clive Swift*); Liz (*Josephine Tewson*); Daisy (*Judy Cornwell*); Onslow (*Geoffrey Hughes*); Rose (*Mary Millar*); Emmet (*David Griffin*); Vicar (*Jeremy Gittins*), Vicar's Wife (*Marion Barron*)

Although the location work for the series generally went smoothly there was a problem during the filming for this episode. For one of the shots towards the end of the chase the car had been rigged by my special effects staff to produce smoke from under the bonnet, which, in the story, results in Onslow having to give up chasing Daddy and pull into a lay-by. Unfortunately, on this occasion, things didn't go quite as planned and whilst the car was belting down the road towards the camera, the tube running between the cylinder in the boot producing the smoke and the bonnet, suddenly burst into flames. The car – driven at this stage by a stunt driver doubling for Onslow – screeched to a halt and Patricia, Clive and Mary leapt out. Unfortunately, Judy couldn't do the same as the tube had somehow been rigged through her safety belt! However, this was rectified very quickly and, thankfully, she only suffered a few burnt hairs. However, there was, understandably, a certain reluctance on the part of the actors to get back into the car for the next shot, and when the car is seen from the rear pulling into the lay-by I didn't bother having anyone standing in for Judy or Mary (because they weren't really seen in that shot) but a member of my team stood in for Richard and I donned Hyacinth's blouse and hat.

I also had to disguise a continuity error. On looking at the rushes I suddenly realised to my horror that in some of the later shots in the chase (filmed on a different day) the luggage rack had accidentally been left off Onslow's car. I got round this by having Onslow say, 'Oh, there goes my roof rack' as the car bumped violently over a bridge!

There were an enormous amount of smaller alterations that I needed to make to the ten episodes in terms of dialogue but if I were to list all these this book would run into several volumes! As well as alterations in dialogue – both in the terminology that Hyacinth would use and to provide some extra humour (a good example of the latter being Hyacinth telling Richard off in the kitchen for making a certain remark by saying, 'Oh, Richard, what a thing to say to someone with a solid-silver self-cleaning sauce separator', which got a very big laugh) – quite a few of the changes I came up with were necessary just to make some sense of a situation.

Apart from Mary Millar joining us as Rose, the arrival of Emmet next door from the second series onwards was definitely a great asset. The inclusion of Elizabeth's brother enabled her to have a confidant, which was absolutely vital and produced same wonderful comedy not only as the two of them discussed Hyacinth but also as Emmet made desperate attempts – albeit not always successful – to keep out of Hyacinth's way. This was a great idea on Roy's part, but then characters and their relationships are his real strength.

The studio recordings also went very well. As a matter of interest the week – or to be more specific, my week – during the rehearsal/recording period went like this:

*Monday:* Read-through and outside rehearsals for next episode to be recorded (10.30 to about 17.00). Then go home with a VHS copy of the episode recorded the previous day and make my notes for the editing session the following day. These have to be very precise and it could very easily take until midnight.

*Tuesday:* Have editing session with Andy Quested. Generally about 09.00 till 16.00. Then catch up with any outstanding paperwork in the office. (This, incidentally, was the cast's day off but they generally spent some of the time learning their lines.)

*Wednesday:* Continue outside rehearsals from 10.30 until approximately 16.30. After this I would return to Television Centre and have a session with Laurie Taylor and Nick Roast tidying up the sound side – where necessary – of the final-edit version of the show which Andy and I had completed the day before. When there had been a lot of retakes (sometimes because of dialogue 'fluffs' but quite often, in the case of Judy, Geoffrey and Mary, because they had 'corpsed' in the middle of a scene!) or when the episode had overrun (generally because of the audience laughter) cuts were required. Whilst Andy had usually been able to edit the sound as perfectly as he did the picture, there were inevitably instances when a degree of 'tidying-up' was necessary. There were also occasions when additional sound effects – music, telephone rings etc. – needed to be added. This session went from 17.00 to 22.00.

*Thursday:* Continue outside rehearsals from 10.30 until 16.30 – by this time the cast would generally be 'off the book' as far as the script was concerned. After rehearsals I would go straight home and work on my camera script (the 'Bible') for the recording of the episode. This meant deciding the position of my cameras for the various scenes and working out which camera should be giving me whatever shots I decided I needed to record each scene. As there could easily be as many as 350 shots in an episode this could be a lengthy process. During the course of this I also needed to mark the positions of the cameras on a plan of the studio sets and exactly where they needed to be plugged into the studio wall to enable them to cover all the sets I planned to use them on, without their cables becoming horrendously tangled on the day. I started work on the camera script as soon as I arrived home and often didn't finish until at least one o'clock in the morning.

*Friday:* Turn up at outside rehearsals in time to give Peter, my production manager, my camera plan so that he could transfer all the information to the 'flimsy' version and take that back to Television Centre to have copies run off for the technicians who would be joining us at 11.30 for the technical run-through. Start rehearsals at 10.30 and use my camera script to check that what I was planning would indeed work with the position of artists relevant to each other, doors, furniture etc. By moving about I also used to indicate to the artists where the cameras would be at any given moment and when I would be taking their reactions to certain things said or done during the action.

At 11.30 the technicians would arrive (lighting director, sound supervisor, sound assistant, designer, props buyer, costume and make-up designers) and Peter would be back in time to give copies of the camera plan to those that it affected – so that they would be able to see exactly where I planned to site the various cameras for each scene. We would then start a run-through so that the people who had just joined us would be able see precisely what would be called for on the recording day in terms of lighting the action in relation to what was going on at any given moment; lighting effects in terms of any lights switched on and off by the artists; where the sound booms would need to be; what sound effects would be required; when telephones would need to ring and which phones needed to be linked so that the artists would be able hear the person on the other end of the line (which always helps!). Also when there would be a recording break and why it was needed – i.e. to enable cameras to be moved, scenery struck or set, or for a costume or make-up change, etc. My production assistant Susan, would also attend this session and she would then return to the Television Centre to type up the camera script.

Immediately after this run-through I would answer any queries the technicians had and then let the artists go and start their lunch whilst I sat down with the technicians and had a planning meeting regarding the following week's episode. For this my set designer would have brought along a plan showing the layout of the sets required for that episode which he and I had previously agreed on. When this was over and I had settled any problems or queries they had, they left and I would rejoin the cast for a quick snack.

After lunch I would continue to rehearse with the cast – generally until about 16.30. I would then either go back to my office at Television Centre to catch up on routine matters or go straight home. Either way I would spend the evening working out the 'blocking' (when and where I would ask the artists to move in relation to the dialogue and what business I would give them in order to get the best out of the script) for the episode we would begin rehearsing the following Monday. I seldom finished this before about 22.00.

*Saturday:* With most episodes Patricia generally liked to continue rehearsing – although sometimes this would only involve the people that she had scenes with. We would start at 10.00 and go on till about 12.30. The rest of the day I was generally able to spend with my wife, Jean, and our two daughters, Helen and Jeanette.

*Sunday:* This was our recording day in the studio. I would get in at about 8.45 in the morning, pick up a copy of the camera script from the print room – where they had been run off overnight after Susan had finished typing the master version – and then go to the studio and check that everything was in order with the sets (which would have been put up during the night) and that the furniture was in exactly the right position to enable me to achieve what I envisaged on my camera script. Even moving a sofa six inches or turning an armchair a few degrees can make all the difference and any adjustments I could foresee at this stage would save time during camera rehearsals.

I would then mark up my copy of the camera script with reminders to myself to cue artists at certain points during the action. In other words, I would write at the appropriate point – perhaps at the start of the scene – 'Q Hyacinth' and then, when Richard had to make an entrance a few seconds later whilst she was in the middle of doing something, 'Q Richard'. During camera rehearsals and the recording I would then call these cues out to my production manager at exactly the right moment and he – by dropping his arm – would indicate to the character in question that this was their cue. I also noted effects like doorbells, telephones, etc. – i.e. 'Q Phone' to tell the sound assistant the exact moment to start the telephone ringing.

By the time I had marked up my script everything in the studio was generally up and ready with all the cameras and sound equipment in position and the lighting supervisor happy that the lights he needed were rigged as he had planned on the basis of attending the technical run-through on Friday. Camera rehearsal would start at 10.30, which involves the artists playing each scene, the cameramen using their camera cards (typed out by my PA and listing each camera's contribution according to my camera script) to offer the shots I had asked for, and the vision mixer cutting from one to another at the point I had decreed in the camera script. We would then go through the same scene again – now that everyone was familiar with what was required – before moving on to the next one.

We would break for lunch at 13.00, resume at 14.00 and generally finish the camera rehearsal at about 16.30. I would then run the pre-recorded (location) sequences so that the cast would be able to see how they had finally turned out. Often, during the dress rehearsal and the actual recording in the evening, they weren't able to see them because they would be in the middle of a costume change. At about 5.15 we would then start the dress rehearsal.

By 18.30 we would finish that and the cast would gather on the audience rostra to hear any notes that I might have for them. After supper they would start to get back into costume and be re-made up for the recording and the audience (of about 320) would be let into the studio around 19.15. On their seats they would find a programme (rather like a typical theatre programme) which listed the various sets that we were going to be using, the name of the artists and their previous credits, and similar information regarding Roy Clarke and myself. In this case there were also a few points of interest about the various studios at Television Centre.

This was an idea which I had started at the BBC many years ago and on which Will Wyatt, the then Managing Director of Television, congratulated me and gave instructions that, thereafter, every show like ours should provide something similar.

At about 19.40 my production manager would go out and introduce the audience to their 'host for the evening' (generally, in my case, the excellent warm-up man Bobby Bragg), who having chatted to the audience for a few minutes would introduce me. I would tell a few jokes associated with the making of this type of television programme, point out the various sets and then introduce the members of the cast to the enthusiastic audience – culminating with Patricia.

I would then go up to the gallery and we would start recording the episode – with the audience also being shown all the pre-recorded location material at the appropriate time in the storyline. Allowing for scene changes, camera moves, costume changes, retakes, and so on, we generally had the show in the can by about 21.30–21.45. As the very happy audience were in the process of departing, I would go downstairs and thank the various members of the crew and go to the costume and make-up areas to do the same thing there and to the dressing rooms to thank the members of the cast. We would then go up to the BBC Club for a quick 'wind-down' drink (and to discuss how the show had gone) before going to our respective homes. The following day everything started all over again on the next episode. Quite a busy week!

Incidentally, American sitcoms seem to have a different way of recording the studio elements. Come to think of it, I don't know why I've said the 'studio' elements because there generally aren't any location scenes. The only exteriors you see tend to be a long shot of a building (the exterior of where the interiors are supposedly located), which is used under a crash of music as a buffer between interior scenes.

Anyway, back to their way of recording the studio scenes. Instead of the vision mixer cutting between the various cameras during the action as per the director's camera script, they tend to record the output of all the cameras all the time. I once met an American director and he started talking to me about the making of *Keeping Up Appearances*, which he liked very much, and he suddenly said to me, 'Wait a minute, are you saying that you cut between your cameras as you go along?' When I confirmed that this was the case he was gobsmacked. He told me that, in America, they arrive at the end result by editing together shots from the various cameras and then they all sit down and watch the show, then throw in their various comments – 'Wouldn't it be better to have the 2 shot at that point rather than the 4 shot?' etc. The piece is then re-edited and they all have another meeting and watch it again. Sometimes there can be as many as half a dozen re-edits and meetings before everyone is happy. I say 'everyone' because over there, as well as the producer and the director, there are associate producers, executive producers, line producers … the list is endless and there are often several people in each capacity!

The man I was talking to then said, 'How do you work out, in advance' (referring to my camera script) 'that you are going to be on the right camera at any given moment?' I responded by saying that having a visual imagination and being able to tell the story with a series of pictures was part of a television director's job. He was even more gobsmacked. Incidentally, although I never did it, there is now a tendency for British directors – whilst still using a camera script to cut between the cameras at the time of the recording – also to record the output of some of their cameras separately and use this as a back-up in the editing process.

At the conclusion of the second series we had the usual end-of-series party but Patricia declined to contribute this time saying that she considered the BBC should foot the bill – a little unlikely as it's not exactly an official 'event', merely an informal knees-up between a group of people who have been working closely together to make the series.

I therefore found it rather embarrassing asking the other members of the cast – although I am quite sure they would have happily paid up. I upped my twenty pounds to thirty and, as, quite by chance, we had a scene in the last episode we were recording (episodes are seldom recorded in the same order as they are transmitted) that involved Hyacinth holding a candlelight supper, there just happened – by a strange coincidence – to be enough items left over to go towards the party afterwards! By an even stranger coincidence it just so happened that, for the next three series the final episode being recorded also involved some form of Hyacinth banquet! Thank heavens it wasn't something that Daisy was supposed to have prepared for a meal round at their place!

On this occasion I thought it might be fun as well as playing the out-takes at the party to also play a fictitious 'sound only' joke telephone conversation involving Hyacinth ringing a man whom, from the content, we realise came round to give her an insurance quote but then the visit became a little more 'friendly'.

I wrote this myself and I can honestly say it was very funny (my PA who typed it out for me thought it was wonderful). My intention was to record it secretly with Patricia obviously playing Hyacinth and with myself playing the man. The content of my script was as follows:

| | |
|---|---|
| HYACINTH: | Humming |
| F/X: | TELEPHONE BEING ANSWERED |
| GIRL'S VOICE: | Fidelity Insurance. Good morning. |
| HYACINTH: | Oh, good morning. My name is Bouquet, that's (SPELLING IT) B-U-C-K-E-T. I'd like to speak to one of your representatives – Mr William Littlejohn. |
| GIRL'S VOICE: | One moment please |
| F/X: | DISTORT SHORT PHONE RINGING. RECEIVER LIFTED |
| LITTLEJOHN: | Hello, Bill Littlejohn |
| HYACINTH: | (IMMEDIATELY 'EAGER') Bill, it's me, Hyacinth. |
| LITTLEJOHN: | Oh, hello, poppet, how are you? |
| HYACINTH: | I'm fine – but can you come round – I'm desperate for another policy. |
| LITTLEJOHN: | Oh, yes, darling, me too. |
| HYACINTH: | How about next Tuesday? |

LITTLEJOHN: Fine, but what about your old man?

HYACINTH: No, it's all right. I've signed Richard up for a series of taxidermy classes.

LITTLEJOHN: Sounds fascinating.

HYACINTH: You do want to come and see me, don't you?

LITTLEJOHN: Yes, very much indeed, Hyacinth.

HYACINTH: Oh, please, there's no need to be so formal – not after last Tuesday – call me 'Cinth'.

LITTLEJOHN: Yes, all right ... 'Cinth'.

HYACINTH: I don't think I'll ever forget that afternoon. 'Let's go through the small print', you said. Ooh, it was wonderful.

LITTLEJOHN: Did the earth shake for you?

HYACINTH: Well, after you left I wondered if we were fully covered for natural tremors.

LITTLEJOHN: Well, I'm glad you were a 'satisfied' customer.

HYACINTH: Oh, yes. How you could have a name like 'Littlejohn', I'll never know.

LITTLEJOHN: Thank you. How are those relatives of yours? Still causing you a few problems?

HYACINTH: I'm afraid so. I don't really like to talk about them but now I know you so well ... Rose, that's my younger sister – the one with the over-active genes – she went to morning service at our church and put a note in the collection plate...

LITTLEJOHN: That was very generous of her.

HYACINTH: ...No, it was a love note for our dishy Vicar – not as dishy as you, of course – anyway the Press have got on to it and there's a piece in the *Binley Woods Echo*. [This was a reference to the real area in which we filmed sequences featuring Hyacinth's home.]

LITTLEJOHN: Oh dear.

HYACINTH: Still, there's some good news as well. Daisy, my other sister, has won the 'Non Housekeeping Award' again – that's the third year running.

LITTLEJOHN: What about that brother-in-law of yours?

HYACINTH: Oh, poor Onslow had a nasty accident. He had to be taken to hospital because he'd passed out.

LITTLEJOHN: Oh dear. What happened?

HYACINTH: Well, he was down at the Employment Exchange and they offered him a job. His fall was broken by a 'six pack' he was carrying but it was still very nasty.

LITTLEJOHN: Yes, I can imagine.

HYACINTH: He made a dreadful dent in the lino. They were quite rude about it. I had to have Elizabeth round for coffee to take my mind off it.

LITTLEJOHN: She didn't break a cup, did she?

HYACINTH: Good Lord no, just a milk jug, two saucers and the spout off the teapot.

LITTLEJOHN: Well, you can claim it on the insurance.

HYACINTH: Oh, Bill – you're too good to me.

LITTLEJOHN: Have you had any more trouble with that man next door?

HYACINTH: You mean Emmet?

LITTLEJOHN: That's the chap .

HYACINTH: No, but it's the same old story. He's always pestering me to sing for him – it's just an excuse to be alone with me. Of course, I daren't let him over the threshold because he makes it quite obvious that be wouldn't be able to keep his hands off me.

LITTLEJOHN: I wouldn't like that, Cinth.

HYACINTH: Oh, don't be silly, Willy, I'll be faithful. I'm yours alone.

F/X: DOOR SLAM

RICHARD'S VOICE: It's only me! [This was going to be lifted from an episode in Series 1.]

HYACINTH: (MORE SECRETIVE) I'll have to go. My husband's back. (A SUDDEN THOUGHT) You don't do life policies, do you?

LITTLEJOHN: Yes, of course we do. Why?

HYACINTH: Just a thought. Till Tuesday. Bye.

Remember, this was to be a sound only recording and the only other person who would have been in on the joke besides Pat and myself would have been my sound supervisor, Laurie Taylor. (The girl's voice would have been my wife's recorded at home and edited in by Laurie.)

Without anyone else seeing, I gave Patricia the script at the end of a rehearsal day in the middle of the final week and explained my plan. She took it away with her. The next day I was amazed (and that's putting it mildly!) when she handed it back and said that she didn't want to go along with the joke.

I was rather surprised because her attitude to what was only going to be an 'in house' bit of fun seemed to be a little inconsistent with that of an actress making her living from comedy.

At the end of the last recording of this series Geoffrey Hughes very kindly said some very nice things about me to the studio audience, then called me on and presented me with a lookalike Oscar which was nice of him. He is, in fact, a very kind man and, over the years we were together, he also gave me a leather belt and a leather 'coaster' both of which had *Keeping Up Appearances* engraved on them.

That year we made our first 'special' for Christmas.

## CHRISTMAS SPECIAL 1991

**Plot:** Hyacinth arranges for Richard to play Father Christmas for a senior citizens' party at the church hall. Over the other side of town Onslow has rather gone overboard in decorating the dilapidated car in their garden. Rose has a new boyfriend who is very romantically inclined and loves dancing.

**Cast:** Hyacinth (*Patricia Routledge*); Richard (*Clive Swift*); Liz (*Josephine Tewson*); Daisy (*Judy Cornwell*); Onslow (*Geoffrey Hughes*); Rose (*Mary Millar*); Emmet (*David Griffin*); Vicar (*Jeremy Gittins*); Postman (*Robert Packham*); Mr Thorgunby (*Mark Brackenbury*); Mrs Thorgunby (*Annet Peters*); Mr Sudbury (*Tony Kemp*); Daddy (*George Webb*)

When we received the original script for this episode it had a final scene (on location outside the church hall) which was totally illogical and, it has to be said, not very funny. When Patricia saw the script she told me quite emphatically that she considered the scene was rubbish and that she wouldn't do it. Christopher agreed with us and rang our writer and very tactfully asked him whether he could come up with a re-write of this scene because we were convinced that the original one 'could be improved'. Sadly, Roy refused to look at it again. I, therefore, found myself in the very difficult position of having a writer who considered the scene was fine but myself, as the show's producer/director, convinced that it was very weak and a star who felt the same – to the point where she was refusing to play in it!

In desperation I went away that evening and wrote a completely new four-minute scene, and when Patricia read it the next morning she remarked that it worked very well and she was extremely happy with it. She asked me to thank Roy for re-writing it and I explained that he hadn't – but, in order to save the day, I had! The scene worked very well and, thankfully, Roy never made any comment – although he told Christopher that he had enjoyed the show. In retrospect, I wonder whether he had just said that and hadn't actually watched it – because, as I mentioned earlier, he told me three years later that he very seldom watched his shows. Besides, if he had watched it, surely he would have noticed a completely new four-minute scene!

Up to now I had often altered things in order to make sense of the original scripts and provided extra dialogue here and there to increase the fun, but this was the first occasion that I had needed to write a completely new scene. Although I certainly didn't realise it at the time, it was not only to be the first of quite a few occasions but also the start of a slightly tricky situation. On the one hand, my boss was going to encourage me to re-write as necessary – because he also wasn't happy with the original scripts but knew that Roy wouldn't do any re-writes – whilst, on the other hand, the BBC was terrified of upsetting him. A rather unfair situation, especially when Ronnie Barker (with whom I had worked on several occasions) had told me a few years later that he quite often used to re-write elements of a Roy Clarke series that he was starring in called *Open All Hours* because the original version wasn't considered to be up to the expected standard. Someone else in that cast and a member of the show's production team recently confirmed that this was the case.

As *Keeping Up Appearances* moved on, I began to realise that our writer, unfortunately, seemed to be quite happy to reuse the same storylines – and, on occasions, almost the same dialogue. Also there were sometimes so many inconsistencies within an episode that you got the distinct impression that, unlike other writers, he probably hadn't sat down and read the whole script after it had been typed up by his secretary.

To finish this chapter on a rather lighter note I must tell you a story concerning Judy Cornwell's liking – passion might be a better word – for certain types of food. Before each new series is transmitted the BBC's Publicity Department holds a 'Press Launch'. Representatives from various newspapers and magazines attend, watch a VHS of one of the new episodes (normally the first one that will be transmitted) and get a chance to interview members of the cast and myself. For our second series this function was held at the prestigious Langham Hotel in London. When the event had finished and people were starting to drift away Judy suddenly noticed that there was a huge pile of beautiful cakes left over. She asked one of the waiters if they had already been paid for and when he confirmed that this was the case she just couldn't resist the temptation to 'remove' them. She was convinced that she had got away with it until she saw Geoffrey Hughes watching her making off with them! Mind you, that didn't stop her. Judy sat in the train down to Brighton (where she lives) eating those cakes.

# Haven't We Done This Before?

Thankfully, the second series was deemed to be a success and it was decided to make a third batch – this time consisting of only seven episodes because of Patricia's limited availability. I wrote to Roy at the beginning of October (giving him plenty of notice) telling him that we needed to have all the scripts by the end of March, six months later. I also mentioned – as tactfully as I could – that I was conscious of the fact that the cast, collectively, were rather worried that there was a distinct feeling of déjà-vu when episodes came up involving either yet another of Rose's men friends or Daddy going missing.

I went on to say that whilst not wishing in any way to teach my grandmother to suck eggs I did rather agree with them that the public who loved the series might start saying, 'We've seen that – can't Hyacinth do something different?'

I tentatively put forward the suggestion that there might be something in us learning that Richard has to take early retirement and we could, therefore, look at the knock-on effects of this. For example, they could have more leisure time together with Hyacinth suggesting – or, to be more precise, organising! – some activity which she and Richard could get up to together.

I also suggested that it might be fun if Hyacinth had the idea of using some, or all, of Richard's golden handshake to purchase a weekend retreat in the country – although he would be far from keen. I said that there could perhaps be three episodes out of the seven where we saw some of their new existence (in conjunction, of course, with their old one). I pointed out that I realised we would need to involve the other regular members of the cast but that wouldn't be difficult. For a start Elizabeth and Emmet could be invited to spend a night and, of course, Daisy and Onslow turning up uninvited would horrify Hyacinth as it would be liable to jeopardise her standing with the 'country set'.

In the event Roy used my idea of Richard having to take early retirement but not the one about the country home – at least not for this series! When the first four scripts arrived I had a number of reservations about the content – as did Christopher. I sent copies of them on to Patricia. A few days later she dropped me a hand written note telling me that she had read Episodes 1–4 four times (each) and that she could barely whip up interest, let alone enthusiasm. She remarked that they were very poor and uninventive and went on to say that she didn't see why we should have to settle for these. She commented that, overall, the scripts were very disappointing and she would ring me later in the week.

She then went on to comment on precise elements of the content of each episode. The majority of her observations coincided exactly with the thoughts that Christopher and I had but, in fairness, there were also a few elements with which we didn't agree. One of the things that Patricia didn't really appreciate until much later in the project was that, whilst it was certainly essential to have good strong new storylines for the episodes, there is always a place in popular situation comedy for a 'running gag'.

For instance, the audience loved Hyacinth's constant problems with Onslow's dog. As soon as she started to go through their garden gate they were waiting for it happen! Incidentally, I went to a lot of trouble to vary the scenes at the gate – it either stuck, fell off completely or came apart in various different ways. They also loved the scenes with Hyacinth and the postman and the milkman and, of course, they were longing to see what happened to poor Elizabeth when she next came round to coffee or Emmet when Hyacinth started to sing at him.

Incidentally, the coffee scenes became more and more difficult because there were so many of them. I recently worked out that twenty-four of the episodes had coffee scenes involving Elizabeth – in some of these episodes there was more than one coffee scene! Although they all revolved around Liz's nervousness – Jo was absolutely brilliant at playing being terrified of Hyacinth, coupled, when appropriate, with a wonderful 'what is she talking about?' expression – I always tried to vary the comedy business I gave her and Hyacinth in order to avoid them doing virtually the same thing each time. The fact that they are both excellent farceurs with a brilliant sense of comic timing certainly went a long way to making these scenes such a success.

When we had received all the scripts for the third series it was pretty obvious that, apart from one (the boat episode), large elements did, unfortunately, cover similar situations that had been used several times before. I still have Patricia's notes to me – by this time having read all seven of the original scripts for this series – asking why they were so patchy and why we should have to settle for 'such carelessly constructed scripts with large elements of the plots exactly the same as we have used before?'

Via Christopher I made various suggestions to Roy and he reluctantly agreed to make a couple of small modifications – although this was only the tip of the iceberg. He denied that there was anything wrong with all the other elements which I, along with Robin Nash, Christopher Bond and Patricia, felt were not up to standard.

A comedy script which isn't very funny is, needless to say, a recipe for disaster. In the world of 'drama' a play can be a number of things – intriguing, exciting, thought-provoking, intellectually challenging, deep in terms of its 'message' – all manner of things. However, in the world of comedy, there is only one real measure of success – is it funny? It is, of course, also important that it should be 'believable', at least to a degree (unless, of course, it's the sort of show that's totally 'off the wall') and within certain levels of good taste, but, on the whole, it needs to be funny and make people laugh.

Christopher and I read the scripts yet again and agreed on the things that really didn't seem to work. Because there was no other option I then did my usual re-writing of various elements of each script. There were a huge number of things I needed to do to all the scripts but I will only refer to the more major problems and the way I got round them.

## EPISODE 1

**Plot:** Richard faces his last day at work and it seems that the prospect of retirement worries him so much that he is in a complete daze. When he finally gets to work he begs to be allowed to stay on – but to no avail. Hyacinth has invited the wife of an influential businessman to tea but her plans to impress her are in jeopardy when one of Rose's boyfriends – whom Rose has arranged to meet there rather than let him see her real home – leaves his huge dog on the drive whilst he pops round the corner for a moment. Hyacinth asks Elizabeth to try and help her shift it.

**Cast:** Hyacinth (*Patricia Routledge*); Richard (*Clive Swift*); Liz (*Josephine Tewson*); Daisy (*Judy Cornwell*); Onslow (*Geoffrey Hughes*); Rose (*Mary Millar*); Emmet (*David Griffin*); Richard's Boss (*Ivor Danvers*); Milkman (*Robert Rawles*); Roger (*Jon Glover*)

The original ending – or 'tag' in the parlance used in show business for the end of a situation – was sadly a perfect example of our writer seeing the 'final picture' in his mind and then, with very little thought about even the most basic logic, writing things so that this 'picture' came to fruition.

Rose's boyfriend left his car (a Dune Buggy) outside Hyacinth's whilst he went down the road to buy some cigarettes. The man leaves Hyacinth the keys but when she asks Elizabeth to move the vehicle for her (because she thinks it is inappropriate to have it outside the Bouquet residence when she is expecting an important guest to tea) Elizabeth can't get the engine to start. Finally, Hyacinth says that she will sit in the car in order to steer it whilst Elizabeth pushes it. Suddenly the engine bursts into life and Hyacinth drives the car down the road (gathering speed all the time, according to the script) and as she is driving along (her hair blowing in the wind, as the script said) she passes the important visitor and waves.

We were expected to believe that the car would have got up to a reasonable speed thanks to the antics of a character who, it had always been established, knew absolutely nothing about driving. If she hadn't had her foot on the accelerator the car would have very quickly slowed down and stopped, and it would never have gone very fast in the first place because Hyacinth wouldn't have been able to change gear – and Dune Buggy's aren't automatic. To my mind it was just too unbelievable. Probably acceptable in the rather more bizarre world of *Last of the Summer Wine* but not in the more realistic world of *Keeping Up Appearances*.

In this instance our writer did agree that it might be a better idea for Rose's boyfriend to leave his huge dog on the driveway. Because Hyacinth naturally wants it moved, she enlists Elizabeth's help as before only to find herself flying down the road as a result of the dog chasing another one. I used a marvellous black Pyrenean Mountain Dog named Lumpa, and the sequence went extremely well and provided a lot of fun. Especially the dog's continuing refusal to obey Hyacinth's instructions to move.

## EPISODE 2

**Plot:** As Richard is no longer employed, Hyacinth arranges a special day out for them both in the countryside – searching for Iron Age remains! Rose is worried about her romantic situation and locks herself in her room and asks for the good-looking vicar to come round and assist her. Daisy asks Hyacinth and Richard to come round and help, and Richard finds himself climbing up to her room to have a look inside – that is, until Hyacinth accidentally knocks against the ladder he is using.

**Cast:** Hyacinth (*Patricia Routledge*); Richard (*Clive Swift*); Liz (*Josephine Tewson*); Daisy (*Judy Cornwell*); Onslow (*Geoffrey Hughes*); Rose (*Mary Millar*); Emmet (*David Griffin*); Vicar (*Jeremy Gittins*); Postman (*David Janson*)

**Additional locations:** Various on Burnthurst Lane, Princethorpe, Rugby

By the way, as you may have guessed, when they were on their walk Richard wasn't up the tree when Hyacinth was talking to him – we merely used a rope to move a branch around and give the impression he was up there.

## EPISODE 3

**Plot:** Hyacinth has arranged to borrow Violet's country home for the weekend. She and Richard haven't been there very long before they meet up with Bunty and her husband, Dorian, who, whilst they are socially in the right class for Hyacinth, are also both extremely eccentric. By the time Onslow, Daisy, Rose and Daddy arrive for a barbecue, as arranged, quite a lot of wine has been drunk and things have rather got out of hand.

**Cast:** Hyacinth (*Patricia Routledge*); Richard (*Clive Swift*); Liz (*Josephine Tewson*); Daisy (*Judy Cornwell*); Onslow (*Geoffrey Hughes*); Rose (*Mary Millar*); Emmet (*David Griffin*); Darian (*Royce Mills*); Bunty (*Marcia Warren*); Neighbour (*Ian Burford*)

**Additional locations:** Country cottage (at Upper Harlestone, Northampton)

The fact that we were going to be filming for this episode was picked up by a local newspaper which told its readers the precise location and date. This worried me because, by now, the series was well known and extremely popular and I just knew that we would have masses of 'onlookers', which, apart from being a nuisance to us, would understandably not go down very well with the owners of the property we were using. Fortunately, it was a paper that was published twice a week and after I had spoken to the editor he agreed to put an article in the next edition saying that because we had experienced some bad weather during the last few days our filming had fallen behind and our plans had had to be changed. We then went ahead and filmed as planned. Sounds a bit devious, I know, but it was the only way to solve what could have been a huge problem.

## EPISODE 4

**Plot:** Hyacinth is furious when she hears about the expensive holiday plans of a local lady and immediately sets about trying to give the impression that she and Richard's plans are far more extravagant.

Things go wrong and whilst Richard goes off to a pub with Onslow she has no alternative but to shelve this particular mission and fulfil her promise to turn up with Elizabeth at a volunteer church-cleaning session.

**Cast:** Hyacinth (*Patricia Routledge*); Richard (*Clive Swift*); Liz (*Josephine Tewson*); Daisy (*Judy Cornwell*); Onslow (*Geoffrey Hughes*); Rose (*Mary Millar*); Emmet (*David Griffin*); Vicar (*Jeremy Gittins*); Vicar's Wife (*Marion Barron*); Waitress (*Karen Chatwin*)

**Additional locations:** Ext. travel agent's (Travel Centre, Regent St, Leamington Spa); int. pub (Heathcote Inn, Leamington Spa); coffee shop (The Regency Fayre, Leamington Spa)

In the original version of this episode the only reason the script had Hyacinth at the church was so that she would be there to witness Rose turning up as a volunteer wearing a skimpy dress in another attempt to ingratiate herself with the dishy Vicar. There was no mention of the cleaning duties that Hyacinth was allocated and both Christopher Bond and myself felt that this was a source of comedy which had been completely overlooked. We suggested to Roy that a lot of fun could be derived from this situation but sadly he wasn't interested.

I therefore wrote the scene myself in which Hyacinth keeps volunteering for various 'posh' duties (arranging the flowers, cleaning the brass, etc.), but is repeatedly overlooked by the Vicar's wife who allocates these jobs to other people. In desperation, Hyacinth volunteers for the next job without even waiting to find out what it is – and, as a result, is horrified to find herself cleaning the church hall lavatories! The scene went extremely well and Roy never said a thing.

There was a very unfortunate 'off-screen' experience when we were filming at the church hall in Northampton. We had moved straight there from Leamington and Mary and Clive had their luggage on the coach with them. Whilst we were filming the driver left the coach for a few minutes and a thief, who, presumably, had been watching for the right moment, stole Clive's credit cards and Mary's jewellery. Clive swiftly cancelled his credit cards but Mary was heartbroken because some of the items were very personal – things that had belonged to her mother and grandmother.

There was a rather more amusing moment when we were in the studio recording a scene between Emmet and Elizabeth. Emmet is playing the piano and Liz turns away from the window saying, 'I thought it was Hyacinth.' The script called for Emmet – ever panicky at the mention of Hyacinth's name – to thump the keyboard. When David, the actor playing Emmet, did so there was a loud crashing noise and both Jo and he glanced under the keyboard and burst into hysterical laughter. The entire front panel of the piano had fallen off!

## EPISODE 5

**Plot:** Sensing that Richard is bored at home, Hyacinth reminds him that he was given a video camera as a retirement present by his colleagues and insists that he goes off and films something interesting. Although he is not particularly enthusiastic about doing so, he as least sees it as a chance to get out of the house, so he goes along with her request. Hyacinth is expecting Councillor Mrs Nugent for afternoon tea and is horrified when Onslow and Daisy turn up outside in their old banger – Onslow in his usual string vest – along with Rose in a very skimpy skirt. She orders them to go but they can't start the car, and Hyacinth is assisting in attempting to push start their ghastly car when Councillor Nugent arrives. As Hyacinth feels that being seen involved in this sort of action – especially with such a decrepit old vehicle and the way the other three are dressed – is not worthy of her social standing, she tells Mrs Nugent that they are rehearsing for some filming which her husband will be doing later. However, she hasn't bargained on Mrs Nugent showing interest and asking if she can also be involved! In the meantime Richard has been arrested and accused of being a peeping Tom.

**Cast:** Hyacinth (*Patricia Routledge*); Richard (*Clive Swift*); Liz (*Josephine Tewson*); Daisy (*Judy Cornwell*); Onslow (*Geoffrey Hughes*); Rose (*Mary Millar*); Emmet (*David Griffin*); Mrs Nugent (*Charmian May*); Policemen (*Jonathan Stratt, Matthew Long*)

**Additional locations:** Richard's videoing (shopping parade in Benson High Street – the phone box was a prop one)

After Councillor Nugent has expressed her interest in being involved the original script called for them to go inside, and later for the front door to be opened to Richard – and the two police constables who were bringing him home – by Hyacinth, Mrs Nugent and Rose not only dressed as tarts but wearing wigs.

Any sensible person – even in the world of comedy – might reasonably ask how Hyacinth, of all people, would happen to have suitable attire available (for herself and two other people), and why on earth would she also, conveniently, be able to lay her hands on three wigs? Being able to do this so readily put the scene into the 'sketch' world.

I achieved the same end result by making it look as if Hyacinth had used normal everyday items of clothing inappropriately on Mrs Nugent and Rose and for them to do things with their hair that was suitably out of keeping. Patricia wasn't keen on getting involved, so I kept Hyacinth out of the 'dressing-up' equation. Roy's original conception was, unfortunately, another example of him seeing a 'final picture' and then conveniently writing things to make it happen.

The farcical business that I gave Hyacinth and Elizabeth which involved them using different doors of the lounge and missing each other was commented on at a high-powered meeting by the then director of BBC Television, Will Wyatt, who is a huge fan of farce. He mentioned that he had noticed lots of farcical business in the various episodes and said to me: 'That wasn't in the script, was it? I assume you put that in.' When I responded in the affirmative he was very complimentary. I subsequently took him and his wife to see the latest Ray Cooney farce and took him backstage to meet the cast afterwards. The three of us and Ray then had supper together.


# EPISODE 6

**Plot:** Hyacinth wants Richard and herself to take an interest in the world of art but unfortunately her plans to visit a local art show clash with Daddy's plans to run away and join the Foreign Legion. Rose and her latest lover start to look for him in the latter's van which is equipped with loudspeakers which accidentally get turned on telling the whole neighbourhood what Rose and he are up to. Hyacinth is horrified.

**Cast:** Hyacinth (*Patricia Routledge*); Richard (*Clive Swift*); Liz (*Josephine Tewson*); Daisy (*Judy Cornwell*); Onslow (*Geoffrey Hughes*); Rose (*Mary Millar*); Emmet (*David Griffin*); Vicar (*Jeremy Gittins*); Mrs Lennox (*Jennifer Daniel*); Mr Finchley (*Nicholas Bennett*); Daddy (*George Webb*)

**Additional locations:** Art exhibition (The Driving Standards Agency Building, Leamington Spa); petrol station (Asda, Chesterton Drive, Leamington Spa)

## EPISODE 7

**Plot:** Hyacinth plans a nautical supper on a boat lent to her by the parents of one of Sheridan's friends. Being Hyacinth, she naturally assumes that it is going to be a magnificent craft and is horrified to discover that it's really a nautical version of Onslow's old banger. She realises that they will have to use it – they've already invited Elizabeth and Emmet – but is anxious that it should be moved away from its present mooring where it looks even worse because it is alongside some very smart and expensive craft. Unfortunately, the process of moving it becomes a nightmare.

**Cast:** Hyacinth (*Patricia Routledge*); Richard (*Clive Swift*); Liz (*Josephine Tewson*); Daisy (*Judy Cornwell*); Onslow (*Geoffrey Hughes*); Rose (*Mary Millar*); Emmet (*David Griffin*); TV Repairman (*Tony Aitken*); Sales Assistant (*Ian Collier*); Youth (*Nicholas Boyce*)

**Additional locations:** Boatyard (Benson Marina); Gentlemen's outfitters (Dunn's, Leamington Spa)

This episode was also interesting. In the original script the tatty boat was moored alongside the river bank a few yards further along from the very prestigious one that Hyacinth at first thinks is the one she will be using. There would, therefore, have been no logical reason for Hyacinth and Richard to go on board the tatty boat, start it up and try and move it away from the expensive one – with the resulting disasters that our writer had in mind – because they could have merely undone the mooring ropes and pulled it further along the bank! They might have had to ease it round other boats but that wouldn't have been too difficult.

Fortunately, my production manager (at that time, John Spencer) and myself found a very helpful boatyard on the Thames where the boats were moored at pontoons, which meant that Hyacinth and Richard *had* to get the tatty boat out into the main river before they could move it further along – which made their adventures whilst doing so, far more believable. This episode – because of the basic need to film on or around the boat – was, at times, quite tricky. As you probably suspected, it wasn't Patricia who tumbled overboard into the water but her very clever stunt double, Elaine Ford. Using a hose, Patricia was then thoroughly soaked for the scene when she met up with Elizabeth and Emmet. Although the stuntman (the excellent Stuart Fell) doubled for Clive in the scene where 'Richard' is pulled into the river, it was necessary later for Clive himself to be seen in the water hanging onto the stern of the boat. To ensure this was safe there was a rope rigged under the surface which Clive rested his feet on. Needless to say, the boat's engine was not used at the time; instead it was towed by another one. Climbing onto this rope, however, turned out to be rather more difficult than had been thought, and when Clive first tried it he disappeared under the surface only to be very quickly assisted by a member of our costume department, Michael, who leapt into the water to 'rescue' him.

The filming for the third series went very well. This time we were staying at the aforementioned Regent Hotel where we were made very welcome. Depending on how many episodes we were doing and, of course, the location content of the particular episodes – always quite high in Roy's Clarke's scripts – we would be away for between four and six weeks. We would work for six out of seven days each week and they would be quite long days. We would leave the hotel at Leamington and drive the fifteen miles or so to our locations –

mainly on the outskirts of Coventry – arriving in time to snatch a quick breakfast from our catering truck (at 7.45) before setting up the lights, camera and sound equipment. We always began filming no later than 9 a.m.

We had lunch – from the same truck – and 'wrapped' (film terminology for the finish of the day's shooting) at roughly 6.30 p.m. before driving back to the hotel. The day started particularly early for the costume and make-up team because, although any artistes that weren't going to be used in the first sequence we were going to be shooting could be made up on location, the ones in the first scenes had to be ready before we left the hotel.

In some cases this could take up to a couple of hours, and in Pat's case nine times out of ten her make-up call would be something like six o'clock in the morning. Mind you, getting her ready seemed to take quite a time – a lot of which she spent 'examining' the results in the mirror. This was particularly tricky when we were in the studio and she had to change from one costume to another and have her make up adjusted a little – or at least checked. Whilst this was going on the studio audience had to wait, and I can honestly say that in all my many years of making situation comedies I have never known anyone take as long as Patricia did to complete a change – despite being assisted by a very talented costume designer, a dresser and a make-up artist.

Obviously, if the change takes too long, there comes a time when you are in danger of losing the audience's attention – even with a good warm-up man chatting to them. During the five years of making the series there were several occasions where I would leave the gallery, go down to the make-up room, open the door and ask them to get a move on. On one occasion I can remember jokingly saying, 'Come on, folks, hurry it up – this is only supposed to be a costume/make-up change, not a sex change!'

Incidentally, when you're out filming, the various scenes required for a series in any one location are all shot in one batch. In other words, you don't film the scenes required at the various different locations for Episode 1 and then go back again later and do the same thing for Episode 2 and so on. For example, any scenes in the entire series which need to be filmed outside Hyacinth's are all scheduled to be shot together over the period of a few days – depending on how many there are. Before we went filming I would have a discussion with my costume designer and we used to agree which of Hyacinth's 'everyday' dresses (as distinct from anything that needed to be 'special') she would wear in each scene. Quite often, therefore, it was possible to have her appear in the same dress for Scenes 6 and 9 of Episode 1; Scenes 8 and 14 of Episode 4; Scenes 5, 7 and 10 of Episode 6 and so on. This meant there didn't have to be umpteen breaks for costume changes, which saved us an enormous amount of time.

Whilst Patricia used to travel out to the location in the morning in the unit coach, at the end of the day I generally drove her back to the hotel, where the lighting director (Bill Dudman), the camera operator (Christopher Kochanowicz), my sound recordist (Morton Hardacre and subsequently Tim Humphries), my VT editor (Andy Quested) and myself used to watch the sequences shot that day – known as the 'rushes' – on video in my bedroom. Patricia used to attend as well and, quite often, Clive.

Incidentally, the reason my VT editor was on location with us was because, as there was so much location material involved in *Keeping Up Appearances*, it made much more sense for him to bring the necessary editing equipment with him and edit the material in his hotel bedroom – cutting it in accordance with my shooting script – shortly after we had shot it rather than us having to keep on sending the tapes back to Television Centre for him to edit there. It also meant that I was able to see the result of his labours on a day-to-day basis rather than wait until I got back to London, which would have meant a delay of about six weeks.

The Regent Hotel had a very pleasant restaurant in the basement called The Vaults, run by Nino, the wonderful restaurant manager. Having had a long and quite tiring day, we didn't always feel like sitting down for a full dinner but there were still quite a few times when Patricia and I would go down to this restaurant.

I can remember the first occasion and the way she couched the suggestion that we should have a meal together. She said that she would buy me dinner and I accepted saying that was very nice of her. We had a most enjoyable meal – the food and service was excellent – and chatted away. Afterwards, I thanked Pat for the meal and we went to our respective rooms to get a good night's sleep before another early start the next morning.

I was a little surprised – and rather amused – when three nights later she suggested that we had another meal together and said that it was my turn to pay! On that occasion, when the wine waiter came to our table I started to order the same house wine that Pat had ordered three nights earlier, only to hear her say, 'Actually I wasn't madly keen on that house wine – why don't we have a bottle of Chablis instead?' You have to laugh!

There was a lot of location filming required for the third series but then it was back to London for the studio elements of the seven episodes. During this series my brilliant props buyer (Sara Grimshaw) added an extra item to the 'junk'-type things that were seen in Onslow and Daisy's living room. It was a red plastic flower device that bobbed around when people near it spoke loudly. Judy and Mary found its antics quite hysterical and there were several retakes required purely because they couldn't stop laughing. After a couple of episodes I had the item removed because it was causing so much merriment that it had became difficult to record any scene in that room without the artistes falling about. Geoffrey then bought one for Judy and one for Mary, which they used to stick on the rehearsal room tables.

It was about this time that I was asked by the BBC to find out whether Patricia would be happy to go for a fourth series. Remembering how patchy a number of the original scripts for Series 3 had been and the fact that our writer had, sadly, done very little to comply with our request for some new storylines, her initial answer was an emphatic 'no'. She now accepted that certain basic elements of the general set-up had to remain but was adamant that the characters had to do something new and she was very concerned – in the light of the two previous series – that Roy wouldn't come up with fresh ideas. She was insisting, not unreasonably, that at least four out of the proposed seven episodes should tread new ground and, if this wasn't going to be the case, she would not sign a contract for a fourth series.

I reported Pat's feelings to Martin Fisher (who had replaced Robin Nash as Head of Comedy), who, from what he had heard, was also rather worried. Twenty-four hours later Martin – whom I already knew because he had previously produced a radio series I had co-written – asked me if I could come up with some possible storylines which he and I could then tentatively put forward to our writer.

Over the next few days I devised nine storylines, including one involving the *QE2*. I also consulted Cunard about the latter because there wasn't much point in coming up with an idea and then finding it wasn't acceptable to them. (You can find the other eight storylines in Appendix 1.) Martin Fisher liked all the ideas very much and asked me to show them to Patricia. She was very enthusiastic and the three of us went out to lunch in the West End to discuss any little points about them. In the event, neither Martin nor Patricia had anything to say to detract from my outlines – although, understandably, both of them had their preferences when it came to which ones they liked best.

The lunch finished with Martin saying that he would contact Roy and arrange for he and I to go up and see him at Doncaster. At long last I was actually going to be able to have what I hoped would prove to he a useful meeting with our writer and I was really quite excited. However, six weeks later – despite my raising the subject a couple of times with Martin – this still hadn't happened. The Light Entertainment Christmas 'do' was upon us and, on meeting up with Patricia there, she asked me when the meeting was going to be. I said that it hadn't been mentioned in the last few days but I assumed that it would now be in the new year. Later in the evening, very annoyed, Patricia came up to me and said that she had been talking to Martin and apparently I wouldn't be going because Roy had said that he didn't want to have a meeting with me – although Martin had never bothered to tell me this!

When I subsequently asked Martin what was happening he said Roy wanted me to *send* him the storylines. Although I would have much preferred to discuss the ideas with our writer personally, I did as I was asked – along with a tactful letter saying that I was only trying to be helpful and perhaps some of them might prove useful. On the 2nd January I received a telephone call from Roy at home (one of only five telephone conversations I had with him in an equal number of years!) saying that he liked the *QE2* idea very much. I was delighted – until he went on to say that he wanted to do the whole series on board the ship!

Not surprisingly, I was somewhat taken aback by this suggestion – after all, it would be a totally different series. By what sort of coincidence would all the regular characters be together on board a liner for seven episodes? And if they weren't all on board – i.e. people like Elizabeth and Emmet – the principal source of a lot of the comedy (which came from the fact that regular characters like these two found themselves in a face-to-face situation with Hyacinth) would no longer be available. I told Roy that I would discuss the prospect with Cunard but warned him that I could foresee difficulties because there was obviously a vast difference between them agreeing to us having our artistes and crew under their feet for four days (the time it would take me to film the sequences for my suggested episode) and the month or so we would need to be on board to film for seven episodes!

In the event – as I knew this would be what Cunard, very reasonably, *would* say and I just couldn't see the basic idea working for seven episodes, anyway – I left it for forty-eight hours and then rang Roy and told a little white lie saying that Cunard, happy as they were to assist for a short period, wouldn't be able to oblige for that length of time.

Three days later, Martin Fisher received a fax from Roy (who also sent me a copy) saying that *Keeping Up Appearances* was over because he would not be dictated to by the show's producer/director as to what the episodes should be about. Part of his message said: 'the fact that it has obviously not occurred to anyone that a writer finds his energy through stepping, perhaps foolhardily, into the unknown shows a massive misunderstanding of the creative process.'

He went on to say: 'the excitement of this process stems largely from stumbling towards enticing shapes and shadows through a fog of mystery.' His fax finished by saying that this element of mystery of exploration – of feeling one's way – 'has, of course, its risks and it can fail more easily than it can succeed.'

What he seemed to be saying – put in rather more down-to-earth terms – was that there was quite a strong chance of a script not being very good but, if that was the case, so be it! I found it very odd that when he had spoken to me on the telephone he hadn't complained about my sending him the *QE2* story (in fact, he had liked it) nor about my sending him the other ideas. But now, for some reason, he had suddenly flipped his lid.

Martin and Jimmy Moir (the then Head of the Entertainment Department) – who was also well aware of all the re-writing I had had to come up with in the past – immediately rushed up to Doncaster to try and sort things out.

Whilst I obviously realised that their mission was to pour oil onto troubled waters I naturally assumed that I would get their support – especially as Martin was well aware that Patricia wouldn't do another series without some new ideas and that *he* had not only asked me to come up with them but had approved of them and asked me to send them to Roy – but I was amazed to discover subsequently that 'support' isn't exactly what I got!

Apparently, Jimmy's opening remark as he came into the hotel room where they had arranged to meet Roy was 'Harold Snoad is a ****'. (I don't really think the word he used should he included in a book of this nature but it started with a 'c', finished with a 't' and rhymed with a type of flat-bottomed boat!)

I subsequently sought Martin's confirmation that this *had* been said and his embarrassed reaction was more than sufficient to confirm that this had indeed been the case. Of course, as far as Roy was concerned, such behaviour not only supported his view that there had been nothing wrong with his scripts but also gave the impression that the BBC obviously wholeheartedly agreed with him that I was in the wrong! It also gives you an idea of the sort of panic that Roy created when he chose to give the distinct impression that he would stop writing a series for the BBC. I was to experience another example of this in January, 1995.

In the event a compromise was subsequently agreed whereby Roy would use my *QE2* idea and come up with three other new ideas so that at least four of the proposed seven episodes would cover 'new' ground. As it happened, my wife and I were going to see Patricia the following night in Carousel at the National Theatre and Martin asked me to put this scenario to her when we met up after the show. This I did, but Patricia, who was very disappointed with Roy's reaction to my ideas, was still far from happy, and it was a quarter to one in the morning when we finally emerged from her dressing room at the

National. In fact, she was still expressing her doubts as we drove her home.

The other three storylines that our writer came up with centred around different elements of the same theme – Hyacinth insisting that she and Richard needed a weekend retreat now that he had retired and their adventures whilst looking for and eventually finding the 'ideal' place. What an extraordinary coincidence that this was exactly the idea that I had mentioned to Roy when writing to him about Series 3!

Around this time Patricia had received an invitation to the Variety Club's Show Business Awards Luncheon at the Hilton Hotel, Park Lane, because – after her performances in *Keeping Up Appearances* – she had been nominated for an award. She very kindly contacted me and asked whether I would like to accompany her. I thanked her and it was arranged that I would get myself to her flat from where we would be picked up by a car laid on by the organisers of the function. I arrived at Pat's at the agreed time: she invited me to share a tipple with her and then the car duly turned up to take us to the Hilton.

As we approached the hotel Pat looked at her watch and, because the journey hadn't take quite as long as the organisers had envisaged, she realised that we were few minutes early. I said that I didn't think it really mattered but Pat disagreed and instructed the driver to continue down Park Lane, round Hyde Park Corner, up the other side of Park Lane, round Marble Arch and then back down Park Lane again. We eventually did this three times!

When we finally arrived at the hotel there were, as is usual on these occasions, a number of photographers outside waiting to take pictures of the celebrities. Just as Patricia and I were about to enter via the glass revolving doors – I was, of course, letting her go in first – there were several requests for her to pose, whereupon she pushed me inside the doors and turned back to the photographers to accede to their request. Unfortunately, whilst posing, she held on to the glass panel of the revolving doors thus preventing me from continuing on inside. As a result, I found myself trapped between two of the glass panels and was thus seen in this situation in the background of quite a lot of the pictures taken. An unplanned bit of comedy business and quite an amusing experience.

The ceremony went very well and it was announced that Patricia had won the award for her brilliant portrayal of Hyacinth, a decision with which I couldn't have agreed more. When she went up to collect it she took with her my place name from our table at the luncheon. During her acceptance speech she graciously held this up – a small piece of card with my name in print not much larger than you are reading now – and said, 'I would like to thank this gentleman for making this award possible.' At first it didn't seem to occur to her that no one could read the card but after a moment or two of people chuckling she obviously must have realised, because she hastily changed her tactics and mentioned me by name. Still, it caused quite a bit of merriment.

After the ceremony as we went out into the foyer it was evident that the same photographers were waiting outside, obviously hoping to get pictures of the various winners emerging clutching their awards. On seeing this, Patricia stopped dead in her tracks and asked for our car to be sent round to the back of the hotel instead. She never told me why she was worried about the photographers' presence – let's face it, they are part of the life of being a 'celebrity' – but I will never forget us being taken through the kitchens of the hotel, to the surprise of the staff, and being smuggled out of a tradesman's entrance into our limousine! I wasn't quite sure if it felt like being a member of the mafia or royalty, although, as I was with Pat, I suppose it was more like the latter! All in all, though, the event was a very pleasant occasion.

# It's Not Getting Any Easier

As the first few scripts for the fourth series started to arrive we discovered that they included a continuing unmarried pregnancy theme, featuring Rose. In one episode Onslow asked her who the father was and she replied that she didn't know but she could narrow it down to a dozen! Whilst I am certainly not a prude, I didn't think this theme was acceptable in a popular family show transmitted at seven o'clock on a Sunday evening. My opinion happened, by chance, to coincide with a general three-line whip from Will Wyatt (the BBC's managing director) which clearly underlined the editorial care that should be taken in such matters. Martin Fisher wrote to our writer expressing his concern, pointing out that whilst it had been acceptable to portray Rose as flighty in previous series it was considerably less acceptable for a family audience to see her pregnant, thereby underlining her promiscuity – especially in an age when AIDS and sexual behaviour are so often in the headlines.

Our writer, however, chose to ignore our views plus the official guidelines and the episodes kept arriving with the pregnancy theme. Finally, I had no other alternative but to remove these elements, which, at times, meant that Rose's contribution would have been a little on the lean side had I not written other material to compensate. While totally in agreement with myself, Patricia and Christopher that large elements of the original scripts were not up to an acceptable standard, Martin Fisher seemed too scared of Roy to back us by using his position as Head of Comedy to ask for the necessary re-writes. Around this time I sent Martin a memo which said:

*'Does my job no longer require me to ensure that the BBC is getting value for money from writers? Am I no longer being asked to ensure that the BBC is not criticised for accepting a weak script which*

83

*has very little logic (not even of the comedic variety) and an obvious reuse of episode ideas?'*

Another note I sent Martin – the first paragraph refers to the episode where the Vicar has electric problems (which we will come to later) – said:

*'One of the scripts sent us didn't make any sense at all. Christopher rang Roy, pointed out the major fault, and he admitted that he hadn't noticed the problem because he had never actually read the end result – he merely dictated it straight onto a tape recorder for typing!*

*'As I told you, Christopher and I have jettisoned two-thirds of one of these very poor episodes and I have written thirty-two completely new pages. However, as you and I agreed, we are not going to tell Roy this. Incidentally, Pat is extremely happy with my contribution. Over the weekend I shall be writing new scenes to try and turn the other two weak episodes into something acceptable, believable and funny.'*

Let's look at the episodes that comprised Series 4. I am not going to mention all of the various elements that I needed to alter (there were far too many to go into in detail), but every so often I will give you an idea of some of the basic inconsistencies in the original versions. Some of these points may appear to be quite small, but they all add up and they still needed to be corrected and the dialogue changed accordingly.

## EPISODE 1

**Plot:** Aware that Richard is missing being at work, Hyacinth happens to see an advertisement in their local paper which says that a large local frozen-food firm, Frosticles, is looking for a managing director. Prestige-wise she thinks Richard is a perfect contender – although he is no way qualified for the job and not really interested. She takes him onto a golf course with a view to him meeting up with the head of the company who, she has been tipped off, plays on that course. She recruits Onslow and Daisy into her plan but, unfortunately, it all goes pear-shaped.

**Cast:** Hyacinth (*Patricia Routledge*); Richard (*Clive Swift*); Liz (*Josephine Tewson*); Daisy (*Judy Cornwell*); Onslow (*Geoffrey Hughes*); Rose (*Mary Millar*); Emmet (*David Griffin*); Millburn (*Frederick Jaegar*); His Companion (*Joe Dunlop*); Postman (*David Janson*); Pillion Rider (*Michael L. Blair*)

**Additional locations:** Golf course (Kenilworth Golf Club)

In this episode there was another reference by Hyacinth to the fact that someone – in this case, Emmet – had made a mark on her hall carpet when she had never had carpet in the hall. From the very beginning – three years earlier – she had always had woodblock flooring but obviously our writer had never noticed this. Only a small point, I admit, but still a little surprising.

In addition to funny dialogue, a huge source of comedy can be gained by seeing the other character's reaction to the lines. In this episode there was a whole scene between Hyacinth and Richard which – according to the original script – we would hear over a long shot of their car driving down a road. I got so much more out of the scene by actually seeing Hyacinth telling Richard her plans for impressing Mr Milburn on the golf course and, equally important, his reaction to these plans.

When describing the final scene of this episode the original script said that the action would happen beneath the closing credits. I found it rather amusing that after three series our writer apparently still hadn't latched on to the fact that the closing sequence was an entity by itself and, therefore, the credits were never superimposed over live action. It only served to support my theory that he seldom – if ever – watched the shows. (He was probably thinking of his series *Last of the Summer Wine*, which does have the credits over live action.)

After Milburn had asked Richard to deal with the two roughnecks on the golf course, we were supposed to see Richard set off towards the yobs only to give up when chased by one of them on his motorcycle. This didn't seem to me to satisfactorily get over the message of Richard suddenly becoming a coward – as was the intention – because most of us would turn and flee if we were in danger of being run down by a motorbike! It seemed more amusing to have Richard start approaching the troublemaker – albeit not very enthusiastically – and then, when he actually meets up with the man and realises just how much bigger he is than himself, to have him turn and run. When Hyacinth strides off purposefully to deal with the other biker I added a line from the latter which showed his confidence and 'strength' prior to Hyacinth dealing with him. In fact, at the dubbing session I did the voice of the biker in this scene.

There were a couple of amusing moments ('out-takes') when we were filming for this episode. When Hyacinth and Richard first arrive on the golf course Richard wants to know what they're actually doing there. Hyacinth's response is to say, 'We're looking for something, Richard.' Pat then tapped her nose to indicate 'secrecy'. Unfortunately, when she did this on the first take, she hit her nose rather too hard and both she and Clive collapsed in hysterics.

There's another moment later on – after Hyacinth has seen Milburn approaching – when things didn't go quite according to plan. Hyacinth is supposed to do a very impressive body swing as she hits the golf ball but she put so much effort into the turn that she lost her balance and completely disappeared out of frame!

## EPISODE 2

**Plot:** Hyacinth wants to spend some of Richard's golden handshake on buying a small weekend retreat in the countryside. Richard is not at all keen but has to show some interest. As he suspected, Hyacinth's idea of 'small' becomes larger by the minute. On the other side of town Rose is thinking of writing her autobiography. At the end of the episode Hyacinth experiences the romantic intentions of a country bumpkin whilst Richard and herself are shown round a cottage.

**Cast:** Hyacinth (*Patricia Routledge*); Richard (*Clive Swift*); Liz (*Josephine Tewson*); Daisy (*Judy Cornwell*); Onslow (*Geoffrey Hughes*); Rose (*Mary Millar*); Emmet (*David Griffin*); Estate Agent (*Denis Bond*); Yokel (*Barrie Gosney*); His Wife (*Liz Daniels*)

**Additional locations:** Ext. estate agent's (Lovitts, Warwick); ext. cottage (at Hampton Lucy, Warwick). We also filmed the living room of the cottage on location but the walk-in cupboard and the bedroom were studio sets.

Apart from modifying the original dialogue here and there, I didn't need to do that much to this episode. I did add Hyacinth's alliterative line: 'Beautiful day, Elizabeth. Completely conducive to contemplating cosy, charismatic, country cottages', which got a huge laugh. Once again, in one of the scenes the original script said we hear Hyacinth and Richard's dialogue over a long shot of the car. Again I altered this. I also added the tag where Hyacinth is chased by the sheep.

# EPISODE 3

**Plot:** Hyacinth is very put out when she hears that the Barker-Finches down the road have attracted a local celebrity to their recent barbecue. She decides that she will have to go one better by doing something different and comes up with the outdoors–indoors luxury barbecue with finger buffet in her dining room. Meanwhile, Daisy is obsessed with the idea that Onslow is having an affair and re-invents herself with a glitzy makeover assisted by Rose.

**Cast:** Hyacinth (*Patricia Routledge*); Richard (*Clive Swift*); Liz (*Josephine Tewson*); Daisy (*Judy Cornwell*); Onslow (*Geoffrey Hughes*); Rose (*Mary Millar*); Emmet (*David Griffin*); C.P. Benedict (*Paul Williamson*); Cashier (*Clovissa Newcombe*)

**Additional locations:** Garden centre (Charlecote Garden Centre, near Stratford-upon-Avon; ladies' hairdresser's (Westgate

Hairfashions, Warwick). The scene in Hyacinth's dining room as it was seen for her outdoors–indoors barbecue was set up on location at the Manor Hall Conference and Training Centre, at Leamington Spa.

There was a funny moment when we were filming outside Hyacinth's for this episode. The action required Hyacinth to hurriedly get rid of Daisy and Rose who had just called in unexpectedly. As she walked them down the drive she was supposed to say, 'You will give my love to Onslow and Daddy.' Instead, when we first shot this element, she said, 'You will give my love to Hyacinth and Daddy', at which point I called out, 'Pat, *you're* Hyacinth!' 'Oh, yes so I am,' she said. Everyone burst out laughing and, as was often the case, Judy was the last one to stop falling about.

## EPISODE 4

**Plot:** Hyacinth volunteers Richard and herself to pick up the Ladies' Luncheon Club celebrity speaker at the railway station only to experience horrendous problems. Daisy tries to get amorous with Onslow, who manages to get away by offering to assist Rose in her new role of selling jewellery door to door.

**Cast:** Hyacinth (*Patricia Routledge*); Richard (*Clive Swift*); Liz (*Josephine Tewson*); Daisy (*Judy Cornwell*); Onslow (*Geoffrey Hughes*); Rose (*Mary Millar*); Emmet (*David Griffin*); Commodore (*Nigel Davenport*); Vicar (*Jeremy Gittins*); Chairlady (*Geraldine Newman*); Committee Members (*Linda James, Liz Edmiston*); Lady at Luncheon (*Ann Davies*); Passenger (*Leonard Lowe*); Station Manager (*Donald T. Allen*); Ticket Clerk (*Gordon Peters*); Lady at Station (*Irene Sharp*); House Owner (*John Barrard*)

**Additional locations:** Railway stations (Leamington Spa and Warwick); ext. of function room (Manor House Hotel, Leamington Spa)

In the original version of this episode Hyacinth planned to use her sherry glasses with the Frinton-on-Sea coat of arms when entertaining the Commodore. I honestly didn't believe that Hyacinth, of all people, would have ever purchased glasses with the name of a seaside resort on them – they might as well have had 'A present from Frinton-on-Sea' written on them. I re-wrote the start of the scene and changed it to her boasting that the glasses were the ones given them when they were invited on board the *Mary Rose*. I then had Richard pointing out that wasn't the case; they hadn't been invited on board the *Mary Rose* – they'd just done the tour – and they had bought the glasses at a charity car boot sale round the back of Portsmouth gasworks!

I wrote Hyacinth's last speech with the stationmaster regarding the mouth organ-playing porter and came up with the business on the platform of Richard taking his hat off to wipe his brow after Hyacinth has sung her sea shanty – only to find people dropping coins into it! In the original version this singing resulted in a slightly down-at-heel Commodore coming off the train and enthusiastically taking Hyacinth away in a taxi (because Richard's car has been clamped) and there then followed scenes in the taxi, a pub and, finally, at the committee rooms in all of which the Commodore behaved in a particularly romantic ('randy' would be a better word) manner with Hyacinth. Since we had already experienced the same thing with the Major in the golfing episode and, in this series, with the yokel whilst looking for the country cottage, I was anxious to keep this element to the minimum and so was Patricia.

I expressed our reservations regarding this aspect to Roy – via Christopher – and also suggested that it might be fun if, whilst they are waiting at the station, Hyacinth and Richard hear that, due to a landslip, the Commodore's train will now be arriving at another station. Then, on discovering that their car has been clamped, Hyacinth spots the Vicar and she insists on him taking them to this other venue. Roy agreed but, unfortunately, having got them to the other station nothing much changed. I wrote the scene with the lady passenger and the one between Hyacinth and the ticket clerk because, in Roy's re-written version, he merely had her dash inside and discover the Commodore, and after that we were back to exactly the same 'randy' scenario as before. All he had done was to delay the romance by a couple of scenes, which didn't exactly solve the problem.

I therefore wrote most of the rest of the episode myself from the point where they leave the first station and altered things so that Hyacinth didn't meet up with the Commodore until she arrived at the function room. For the final scene in the Vicar's car I used Roy's dialogue from one of the earlier scenes of his that I had dropped. Patricia was much happier with my version.

It was quite interesting filming at Leamington station. I knew that as soon as a train pulled in and the (real) passengers started to get off and walk down the platform towards us they would spot Patricia, Clive and the film unit and, inevitably, look towards the camera and point us out to their companions. To get round this, I employed ten extras to stand on the platform as the train came in – one every five yards or so. As the real passengers got out they joined them and asked them to behave naturally and not to look at the camera. This worked very well.

Obviously, you can't expect a train to wait in the station whilst you complete all the shots in the sequence so we actually used three different trains to achieve the end result. I hope nobody noticed that the windows in one of them were not quite the same as in the other two. That's just a secret between us – don't tell your friends!

There was an amusing moment in the kitchen scene where Hyacinth is putting Emmet's coffee down on the table. Unfortunately, as she did so, she tripped over one of the three 'feet' of the table and we had to do a retake. Emmet was lucky he didn't finish up with the coffee all over him.

## EPISODE 5

**Plot:** Richard has to go to the local police station to retrieve Daddy whilst Hyacinth enlists Elizabeth's assistance to continue her search for a suitable country retreat. In the light of his experience of their previous search for a property, Richard is very concerned that Hyacinth is going to show too much interest in something out of their league, which, when he eventually meets up with her, turns out – at first glance – to be exactly what she is doing.

**Cast:** Hyacinth (*Patricia Routledge*); Richard (*Clive Swift*); Liz (*Josephine Tewson*); Daisy (*Judy Cornwell*); Onslow (*Geoffrey Hughes*); Rose (*Mary Millar*); Emmet (*David Griffin*); Constable (*John Phythian*); Eric (*Terence Hardiman*); Estate Agent (*Jennifer Clulow*); Sir Edward (*John Arnatt*); Sergeant Watkins (*Eric Carte*); Driver (*Stuart Fell*); Daddy (*George Webb*)

**Additional locations:** Ext. police station (Leamington Spa police station); ext. country mansion – 'Marston Hall' (Parham House, Pulborough); 'Marston Hall' gates (gates of Honington Hall, Shipston-on-Stour)

The main location requirements for this episode called for a large country mansion in which Hyacinth eventually buys a bijou flat and the impressive gates which Hyacinth spots as Elizabeth drives past. Peter Laskie (my new production manager) and myself had already found the mansion (near Southampton – an area we were going to be in for Hyacinth missing the *QE2*) but that property didn't really have impressive gates. We therefore used the gates of another property for the arrival sequences.

When the estate agent arrives late for her appointment to meet Hyacinth and Elizabeth at the mansion her excuse is that the road leading up to the house has been blocked by someone's car – at that time she doesn't know it is Elizabeth's. Sounds simple enough, but given the fact that the property we were filming at needed to be huge and in the middle of the countryside, it didn't have a formal drive with landscaped flower beds either side, and, of course, *had* it been that type of property, the drive would have been much shorter and it certainly wouldn't have taken the estate agent at least ten minutes to walk from her abandoned car as her dialogue in the script said.

In reality, the 'drive' was merely a long road through a vast area of grass – and, therefore, it wouldn't be that difficult for the estate agent to pull off the road and drive carefully round the other car. Suddenly the answer came to me. Halfway along to the property the road went over a narrow bridge crossing a river, so when Elizabeth drives back to let Hyacinth have another look at the long-distance view of the mansion (as was Roy's original intention) I had her tell Elizabeth to stop the car right on the bridge – because she felt this was the place from which they could get the best view of the property – and then to leave it there whilst they walked back to the house. I showed Elizabeth looking suitably concerned about leaving the car there but obviously feeling, as usual, that she had better not argue with Hyacinth. In that position it obviously *did* block the road.

One logistical problem I had with this episode was the fact that Judy Cornwell was on the last part of a tour with a play during the first two weeks of our filming, so I had to arrange things so that certain location elements of both this episode and Episode 6 could be filmed to fit in with this. For a few days she doubled between filming scenes such as those outside Onslow's – any needing Daisy being done in the morning – and then, whilst we carried on with scenes that didn't involve her presence, she drove over to Coventry for her evening performance in the play. This plan also worked well for the scene outside the gates of the mansion (which, as I said earlier, had no connection with the house) but filming of the scene outside the actual mansion with Onslow, Rose and Daddy was a little more difficult.

This took place on a Monday and Judy was only able to be there for a short while because, in this case, she had to drive from much further south – as I said we were filming near Southampton – to her next theatre which was, again, up north. However, everything went according to plan and before she had to dash off I managed to film all the shots in which we definitely needed to see Judy. However, in the shot of Onslow and Daisy looking at the property – with Onslow pointing at it – my wonderful props buyer, Sara Grimshaw, stood in for Judy – with suitable padding! I needed this shot as a 'buffer' so that the viewer would find it believable that Richard (whom they had last seen in the middle of the quadrangle talking to Elizabeth and the estate agent) had the time to be able to get to Hyacinth who is on the edge of the quadrangle.

Incidentally, on the subject of padding… Whenever Patricia had to have a stunt double – for example, falling into the river in Series 3, changing position with Richard in the rowing boat in the dredger episode in the Series 5 and horse riding in this series – the double needed to have padding in order to match Patricia's 'slightly' larger figure. This was very carefully supervised by my excellent costume designers, Rita Reekie and then Laura Ergis, and the double always finished up looking identical to Hyacinth. Patricia, however, never accepted this fact and insisted that the padding was reduced – sometimes to the point where the double looked almost sylphlike!

Incidentally, throughout the whole five series my costume designers came up with some wonderful designs for Hyacinth's wardrobe which not only brilliantly illustrated a vital aspect of her character but, on some occasions, added comedy in their own right. As I mentioned earlier, *Keeping Up Appearances* was extremely popular in America. Apparently some people hold 'theme' parties which require guests to turn up as the various characters. I once received a letter from an American doctor who was attending one of these functions and wanted to know where he could get an Onslow-type vest!

One interesting little point about Judy's theatre tour was the fact that the character she was playing on stage required her to speak with a New York Jewish accent, which was a long way from the voice she used for Daisy. When we came to film her first contribution for this series – outside the church hall at Northampton – she had an enormous problem finding 'Daisy' which, at first, was very funny. After a few retakes, however, and with time not on our side, I began to get quite worried. Thankfully, the matter was solved when Geoffrey Hughes took her aside and they started to chat together 'in character'.

Anyway, back to the mansion episode. Whilst you would believe – as was the intention – that the scene between Hyacinth, Sir Edward and the estate agent was filmed in part of the main house, it was, in reality, shot in a conservatory which stood totally on its own three hundred yards away from the house.

Most writers – certainly all the others I've ever worked with – have a pretty good idea of the basic practicalities of making a television series and automatically take certain things into consideration when writing a script. Unfortunately, our writer seemed to be unaware of these practicalities (possibly because he seldom, if ever, attended a studio recording). When the original script arrived it contained a scene in Onslow and Daisy's living room which consisted of just three speeches. That was the only scene in the whole episode that needed that set, so we would have had to get it out of the scenery store, transport it to the studio, put it up, dress it with all the furniture and usual junk, take it all down afterwards and put it back in the scenery store – all for just twelve seconds of screen time!

We already needed to have sufficient space in the studio for Hyacinth's hall, Onslow and Daisy's bedroom, Liz's lounge, and the interior of the police station, without having to include another set which would be used for such a short scene. I changed it so that it happened on location outside Onslow's as Richard was in the process of leaving. This was no problem as we had other scenes to do there – it just took us another twenty minutes or so and that was that.

## EPISODE 6

**Plot:** Richard's initial fears about the size of the place that Hyacinth has found in the country have been eliminated because, to his immense relief, their flat is only a very small part of the mansion. The sale has gone ahead and they are in the process of moving in and realising just how minute the place is. Hyacinth's first priority is her desire to meet up with the 'country set'. They have invited Elizabeth and Emmet down to see the place and, in the meantime, Hyacinth has decided that she and Richard should be seen by her neighbours to be dressed as if they are going riding – although they have no intention of doing so. However, not only does she find herself obliged to ride a horse but the Onslow clan turn up out of the blue and let the side down. As if she didn't have enough problems with Emmet getting his head stuck through the sloping ceiling!

**Cast:** Hyacinth (*Patricia Routledge*); Richard (*Clive Swift*); Liz (*Josephine Tewson*); Daisy (*Judy Cornwell*); Onslow (*Geoffrey Hughes*); Rose (*Mary Millar*); Emmet (*David Griffin*); Postman (*David Janson*); Milkman (*Robert Rawles*); Visitor (*Helen Darward*)

**Additional locations:** Ext./int. country mansion (Parham House, Pulborough); stables (Warwick International School of Riding, Guys Cliffe, Warwick)

In this episode there was, regrettably, another example of 'impracticality' – not something that you, the viewer, would think about but something of which most writers would be aware. In the previous episode we had met another resident in the flats – Sir Edward, as I mentioned earlier. He had played a reasonably lengthy dialogue scene in the conservatory and had subsequently been involved with Hyacinth when she was pushing him around in his wheelchair. In that episode he had been an actor playing a speaking role and had been contracted and paid accordingly. In this episode the character of Sir Edward had no dialogue and was merely seen very fleetingly on just two occasions. All he had to do was to turn when Hyacinth called out to him and then hurriedly make himself scarce by darting round a corner. His contribution in this episode had, therefore, been reduced to that of the category 'Walk On' – or, more appropriately in this instance, 'Dash Off'! Hardly the sort of contribution that an established actor would have been happy to have made and certainly not worth the sort of fee which the BBC would have had to pay him!

The original version of this script contained same farcical scenes in the studio which involved Hyacinth climbing in and out of a very small window of the flat (which was supposedly on the top floor and adjacent to a flat roof) several times and at great speed in the process of hiding from visitors. I thought this was extremely impractical and Patricia was certainly dead against it. I was pretty sure that our writer had assumed Patricia would be quite capable of doing this after seeing her climb over a garden wall in the episode in the first series. This is what I said in my letter to him:

*'Patricia and I have discussed the practicalities of Scenes 31 and 33 and, as I suspected, she is not at all happy. There is a vast difference between what you have written here and her being seen climbing over a wall on location. For a start she never actually climbed the wall at all – I shot her 'progress' in three separate shots – all she did was put one leg up on the wall (cut), I then sat her on the wall, got her to lean sideways and then straighten up (cut), put her over the other side of the wall with one leg still to bring over and that was that. Put it all together and (with the bridging*

*shots of people at the window) it looked as if she had climbed the wall. This, new material on the other hand, is a long scene played in front of a studio audience – as practically all interiors are. Climbing in and out of a relatively small window (it would have to be small to make it believable that she could get stuck) at what has to be at a minimum height of about 2 feet 6 inches at speed is frankly dangerous. If she falls and, at the minimum, breaks an ankle – the rest of the series is in jeopardy.*

*She is, of course, also not of a particularly slight build and is in her mid sixties. I think to attempt this would be extremely foolhardy and there is certainly no point in being wise after the event. I would be grateful if you could come up with something else.'*

On this occasion Roy agreed and suggested that it was changed to the business of her hiding in a very small cupboard. This worked very well. I mentioned earlier that Pat had a stunt double for the riding scene. I achieved the initial, closer, shot of her shooting out of picture as the horse took off by sitting her on the camera dolly and then having it (and her) pulled through the frame.

Fans of the series might be interested to know that the first staircase Hyacinth and Richard went up – the wide one with the huge mirror at the bottom – wasn't shot in the mansion location (because they didn't have anything impressive enough) but was actually filmed at the Regent Hotel where we were staying.

This was another episode which originally concentrated a great deal on Rose trying to tell Hyacinth that she was pregnant – although not really sure who the father was. As I said earlier I had removed all this element so major re-writes were needed to ensure that the episode would finish up the right length. I wrote the scene in which Hyacinth surveys the beds in their tiny new bedroom – apart from the final five speeches. I needed a time-lapse 'buffer' scene at Daisy's and, since I couldn't use the original one because it was all about Rose's pregnancy, I wrote the scene where the ever romantic Daisy brings Onslow some cocoa in their bedroom – only to find that he is already fast asleep!

I also added a great deal to Hyacinth's attempts at riding (one example being her surprise when Richard walks round to the other side of the horse when she thinks he's holding up her legs whereas, in reality, he has merely rested them on a stable door) and to the scenes where Elizabeth and Emmet go back to the flat later and, much to Hyacinth's horror, Onslow, Daisy and Rose also turn up. It was also my idea that the episode should finish with Onslow and Daisy getting stuck between the worktops in the kitchen. With two such conspicuously well-built actors it seemed an obvious move. In fact, after we had recorded the scene where Hyacinth and Richard get stuck, we had to open up the gap between the two surfaces a bit more to enable us to get Onslow and Daisy in there at all!

In the original script for this episode Onslow and Daisy arrived at the country mansion making all sorts of remarks which clearly indicated that they were seeing the outside of the place for the first time – when we had already seen them there in Episode 5!

One amusing moment is this episode was when Hyacinth and Richard are first seen in their riding gear. As they arrive at the car Richard says, 'I can't wear these and a horse', to which Hyacinth replies as she opens the car door, 'We don't actually have to ride.' On the first take she added the line still in character as Hyacinth, 'Could the car door be unlocked, please?' Unfortunately, she was right. This hadn't been checked and it was, indeed, locked!

## EPISODE 7

**Plot:** Hyacinth has volunteered Richard's services to fix a fault with the electrics in the church hall. He is none too keen as, understandably, he doesn't think that he is qualified to do the work. Anyway, he goes under the stage to do what he can and finds the Vicar who is hiding from Hyacinth. Eventually, they are joined by Onslow and Emmet, also both anxious to escape. Richard's attempt to solve the electrical fault doesn't exactly help the bring-and-buy sale which is being held in the church hall.

**Cast:** Hyacinth (*Patricia Routledge*); Richard (*Clive Swift*); Liz (*Josephine Tewson*); Daisy (*Judy Cornwell*); Onslow (*Geoffrey Hughes*); Rose (*Mary Millar*); Emmet (*David Griffin*); Vicar (*Jeremy*

*Gittins*); Vicar's Wife (*Marion Barron*); Postman (*David Janson*); Mrs Drummond (*Sue Lloyd*); Driver (*Pamela Abbott*); Daddy (*George Webb*)

The original script for this last episode of the series was really quite odd. We learned that Hyacinth had volunteered Richard's services to solve a problem with the electrics at the Vicarage. Why the Vicar couldn't just call in an electrician like anyone else I don't know, but let's look at it a bit further. Having got Richard to go to the Vicarage, the script then had four other women plus Liz, Emmet and a prestigious lady from up at the Grange (Mrs Drummond) all turn up there as well and, as there was no other reason given, one was left with the distinct impression they must also have called in to help fix the Vicar's lights!

I asked Christopher to enquire whether our writer had left some element out – such as the women actually turning up for a church function. I also suggested that it might be a better idea if the fault was with the church hall lights instead of the Vicarage's, which would give more of a 'community' reason for Richard helping.

In this instance Roy agreed and said that he would send me some pages that would (a) make this change and (b) make sense of the other people turning up – such as a church bring-and-buy sale.

However, when the re-write turned up, there was nothing about the bring-and-buy sale, merely four pages of Hyacinth asking a small boy in the church hall car park to assist her in trying to determine the sexuality of Mrs Drummond's dogs! It was at this point that I gave up – especially as time wasn't on my side – and I re-wrote large chunks of the episode myself, including all the material relating to setting up the bring-and-buy sale. In the original version of this episode nothing very much happened – the electrics' theme was completely forgotten and was replaced by more material about Daddy getting lost and finished with Hyacinth walking Mrs Drummond's dogs and finding Daddy dragging their owner into the bushes for a bit of slap and tickle. I therefore wrote all the material which culminated in the explosion.

There were a lot of other inconsistencies during the series – the original scripts referred, for example, to Hyacinth and Richard going up and downstairs, although they live in a bungalow (the type of property that our writer himself had originally requested), and to Hyacinth looking through her kitchen window and seeing people arrive at her front door when even the viewers could have told our writer that her kitchen is at the rear of the property!

Incidentally, a couple of weeks after we were in possession of the original scripts for the seven episodes required for this series, Christopher mentioned to me that in a conversation he had just had with Roy, he had got the distinct impression that the latter was getting suspicious that we hadn't asked for any further re-writes. Quite funny really – on the one hand, he didn't want to know about any requests for re-writes but, on the other hand, if he wasn't asked to do any he still wasn't happy! I decided that I had better write to him and try and clear the air:

'*Dear Roy, I understand from Christopher that you are concerned that elements of the scripts you have sent us for this series have been rejigged. This presumably stems from the fact that – apart from the church hall/electrics episode – I haven't asked you for any re-writes.*

*I will explain why this is. I suppose it all started with the Christmas episode eighteen months ago when we asked you for a new ending because no one thought it worked. Regrettably, you refused to re-write it and I had no alternative but to come up with something different, which everyone agreed worked much better. Although it differed considerably from your own version I assumed you eventually approved because, when asked by Christopher, you said you had enjoyed the show.*

*In the last series I was very unhappy with certain elements of Episode 2 and, in my capacity of producer/director of the series – and, therefore, with the overall responsibility for editorial control and ensuring that we maintain strong episodes – I asked Christopher (who agreed with me) to request that you re-wrote certain elements. You declined to do so and I, therefore, amended these myself.*

*As you know when it came to this current series Patricia Routledge (on the strength of your scripts for the third series and elements of the second) was getting somewhat concerned that we were in danger of repeating things that we had done (in some cases, more than once) in the past. I am not referring to running gags like Onslow's dog; I mean episode ideas.*

*With this in mind – and because I knew you had a lot on your plate – Martin agreed with Christopher and myself that it would be a good idea if I wrote some outlines which you might find useful. You wouldn't agree to let me come and see you and I was therefore obliged to send them to you. In my letter I very carefully said that I was only trying to be helpful – you didn't have to use them but you might find them useful. Your reaction was to refuse to write the series at all!*

*We got over that and then your scripts for this series started to arrive. We felt there were considerable problems with some of them. Particularly the episode when Hyacinth volunteers Richard's services to solve the problem the Vicar was having with his electrics at the Vicarage. Having got Richard there you then had four other women plus Liz, Emmet, and the prestigious Mrs Drummond all turn up to try and fix the Vicar's lights. Even with comedic licence, we found that extremely unlikely and I asked Christopher to enquire whether you had left an element out – such as the women actually turning up for some church function. As I understand it, you agreed that it would be a better idea if we changed it to the church hall lights (less personal to the Vicar than his home and more of a 'community' ring to Richard helping) and said that you would send us some pages that would make sense of the other people turning up – such as a bring-and-buy sale.*

*As your re-write only consisted of yet more pages of Hyacinth with Mrs Drummond's dogs, it was at this stage that I felt that perhaps I was right and that you had too much on your plate, and I started to work on the scripts in order to assist – especially as time wasn't on my side.'*

As I rather expected, I received no response to this letter.

Overall in the fourth series plus the *QE2* special – which we'll come to in the next chapter – I not only did a considerable amount of re-writing but also added a lot of new material of my own to replace the original elements which it was considered wouldn't work. I had to get this done on top of all my normal duties as the producer/director, which was a nightmare. To achieve this I was working seventeen-hour days, seven days a week for six weeks. When I turned up on location for the first day's filming members of the cast were appalled at how tired I looked and were really concerned about me.

I had put myself through hell out of loyalty to the BBC and to the series. In short, I knocked myself out ensuring that *Keeping Up Appearances* kept up its appearances! Incidentally, it should be remembered that I was never paid a fee for any of the material that I wrote. I also wasn't on a contract that paid me 'overtime'. I had an annual salary and that was it – however many hours I worked.

The location filming and the studio recordings went very smoothly and, as before, the series was extremely well received. I still had Susan as my PA – she was brilliant – and my new production manager, Peter Laskie, was wonderful. Both of them stayed with me until the very end of the project – the 1995 Christmas Special.

Incidentally, around this time, Geoffrey, Judy and Mary had taken to bringing in Walkmans so they could listen to music in the rehearsal room when they weren't involved in scenes. At some stage Geoffrey introduced them to Irish jig-type music and the three of them would sit round a table swaying to the rhythm. I think Patricia thought they were crazy. Come to think of it, she could have been right!

For some time now the members of the cast and myself had been regularly receiving hundreds of letters from viewers in the UK and overseas, saying how much they were enjoying *Keeping Up Appearances*. Around this time someone who had just returned from a holiday in northern France sent me a photograph she had taken of a road sign which said 'Rue Hyacinth Bouquet' – which is quite an honour.

# All Aboard for a Special Episode

## SPECIAL EPISODE

**Plot:** Hyacinth and Richard take a cruise on the *QE2*.

**Cast:** Hyacinth (*Patricia Routledge*); Richard (*Clive Swift*); Liz (*Josephine Tewson*); Daisy (*Judy Cornwell*); Onslow (*Geoffrey Hughes*); Rose (*Mary Millar*); Emmet (*David Griffin*); Postman (*David Janson*); Check-in Girl (*Alice MacDonald*); Ship's Officer (*Michael Cochrane*); Restaurant Manager (*Bernard Holley*); Holidaymaker (*Barry Bethell*); Port Official (*Mark Brignal*)

**Guest appearances:** The Band of the Welsh Fusiliers; Lindsay Frost; The Mark Joyce Showband; Lord Lichfield

**Locations:** The *QE2*; Southampton Docks; Southampton Airport; Oslo Docks

The idea that I had put forward involving the *QE2* revolved around Hyacinth and Richard having paid a lot of money for a cruise and Hyacinth, being her, expecting all the 'first class' treatment – dining at the Captain's table, etc. – only to discover, to her absolute horror, that Onslow and Daisy are on board (they had won a competition, although Hyacinth doesn't know this at first) – and, because of this, they are getting all the red-carpet treatment she had automatically assumed would be coming her way.

However, when the script turned up our writer seemed to have gone out of his way to steer clear of my suggested storyline as much as possible. Things were very different and also a little difficult to believe, or – in view of the nautical theme of the episode – 'take on board'!

For a start, on the same day that Onslow and Daisy were going down to join the *QE2*, Onslow still managed to find time to take her round to Bruce's with him to try and sort out a problem that Violet and Bruce were having with their drains! Also having dealt with the drains they still managed to get to Southampton before Hyacinth and Richard! A somewhat unlikely scenario in view of the fact that Onslow and Daisy would have had a lot of other things on their minds – such as packing, getting into reasonable clothes and driving all the way from the Midlands down to Southampton Docks.

Far more importantly, Roy had also changed things so that Bruce has paid for Onslow, Daisy, Rose and Daddy to go on the cruise and it was Hyacinth who had won two tickets, which completely destroyed the whole point of my idea of her nose being put out of joint when she discovers Onslow and Daisy are honoured guests.

Christopher tactfully explained this to our writer and, thankfully, on this occasion, he did agree to do a re-write so that Onslow and Daisy had won the cruise. When I had come up with the idea for the episode I had given it to Roy in some detail, including possible locations at the port and on the ship – and my storyline suggested events that might happen in those areas. To arrive at this, I had met up with Cunard's very helpful corporate communications manager, Eric Flounders, who had given me a tour of the ship whilst she was in Southampton Docks between cruises. I had done this research and passed the information on to our writer in order to help him.

For some reason he still chose to ignore a number of the excellent possibilities on offer and Martin Fisher totally agreed with me that if we were lucky enough to be filming on one of the world's most famous liners, it was foolish not to take advantage of what the ship had to offer and that I had better change it as necessary to make it a 'fuller' project.

With Martin's approval, therefore, I wrote a number of scenes utilising the various missed possibilities – the observation gallery at Southampton Docks, the departure lounge there, the bridge of the *QE2*, the ship's Grand Lounge and so on. I also increased the number of problems Hyacinth and Richard had in getting to Southampton on time.

In the original script Hyacinth merely gives Richard two wrong directions as a result of which they finish up in a field. We felt that this would be unlikely to make them that late – especially as Hyacinth, being Hyacinth, would obviously have ensured that they erred on the side of caution by leaving home early.

With this in mind I built in other delays such as having them get held up on a motorway and a level crossing, and arguing about the route, so that Richard fails to notice that they are driving into quite a deep ford, from which they need to be towed out.

By the way, the deep ford was not really a ford. When I had been searching for locations for an episode in Series 2 (the one with the chase sequence after Daddy had pinched Richard's car), I had noticed a dip in a country road which I could imagine could be turned into a ford. On both that occasion and for the *QE2* episode, plastic sheeting was put down along the sides and then the local fire brigade flooded the area. We contributed to a charity of their choice as a reward for assisting us; they said they found it rather more interesting than cleaning cars, which they sometimes did to raise money for charities, though it was strange for them to be asked to flood somewhere because, normally, they only have requests to drain an area!

For this episode I filmed Richard's car being towed out by a farmer's tractor but, unfortunately, I had to drop this sequence when it came to the final edit because the episode was running too long. Incidentally, it was quite interesting arranging the sequence where Hyacinth's car is seen in a traffic jam on a busy motorway. We have all experienced being caught in traffic jams but when you're up to your eyes filming a number of different sequences in the same day there is no way that you can drive around in the hope of finding one! The obvious answer was to create our own, and during our location recce Peter Laskie and myself drove around looking at several roads in an area where we had already found the large country house in which Hyacinth would buy her 'bijou' flat. We needed a road that looked fairly major – and also, of course, the heavy traffic that would be using it – but we had to choose somewhere that wouldn't result in total chaos when we brought everything to a stop. We eventually found the ideal road for our purposes – it looked like a motorway – and then went to see the local police, who were very helpful and agreed to my plan.

Namely, that during the filming there would be a prominent notice across the back of Hyacinth's car which said in large letters: 'Filming for *Keeping Up Appearances*. We will only delay you for one minute. Many thanks'. The camera was already mounted on the bonnet of their car which, as usual, was being towed by a Range Rover, with the cameraman and myself in the back watching the picture on a monitor and, with myself and the sound recordist listening to the dialogue on a pair of headphones. Also on board was my wonderful production assistant, Susan, whose job during the location filming was to take a note of the shot numbers and reasons for any retakes and to watch out for any continuity errors.

At what I felt was the appropriate moment we pulled up and, of course, everything behind us had no alternative but to do the same. The road had three lanes so two of our own vehicles were alongside Hyacinth's so that those two lanes were also blocked. I had already rehearsed Patricia and Clive with the dialogue whilst we had been driving down the road so, thankfully, they were able to do it in one take. We actually only stopped the traffic for slightly less than a minute before everyone was on their way again.

The end result worked very well. And no one waved at the camera! I would liked to have established their car in a wider shot of the traffic jam but, as I only had the one camera – and this was mounted on the car bonnet – this wasn't possible.

When I had originally put the *QE2* idea forward I suggested that Elizabeth and Emmet should decide to drive down to wave them goodbye (Emmet anxious to ensure that Hyacinth actually went!) and also that Hyacinth should telephone the bridge of the *QE2* to ask why the ship has left without her and then ask them to go back for her. The latter was certainly a funny idea. However, for some reason the original script ignored both these suggestions so I went ahead and wrote the respective scenes myself.

Although I had very carefully informed Roy that there are no crowds on the dockside when the ship leaves – any family and friends watch the departure from an observation gallery at a much higher level – he still supplied directions in his version saying, 'Hyacinth bulldozes her way through the crowds to the quayside'. Instead, I managed to talk the military band into letting her rush through their ranks as they marched along playing.

Also in my original storyline I had suggested that when Hyacinth telephones the bridge, a ship's officer could casually come up with the idea that she could catch them up by flying to Copenhagen, whereas in Roy's version – where there was no scene involving the bridge – they merely turned up at Southampton Airport. This meant we would have completely missed seeing Hyacinth's change from despair to extreme excitement when the officer makes this suggestion – and we would also miss quite a few laughs, as well as the chance to give the episode some realism by involving the real *QE2* bridge. As I have mentioned, I wrote the missing scene – including Hyacinth's initial response to the officer's suggestion that she could catch the ship up – namely: 'Now listen to me, my good man. Important as I am in local circles I have not yet risen to the level where I can walk on water!', which got a huge laugh. In the original version we then merely saw Hyacinth arrive at the ticket desk at the airport, ask for tickets and hand over their luggage. I added the security questions that the ground hostess asks (and would have had to ask) and Hyacinth's misunderstanding of the questions, thereby creating some extra fun.

Although it was Roy's idea to have Hyacinth and Richard tour the ship posing as joggers in their search for Daisy and Onslow, that was all he actually said. There were no suggestions as to what this might involve and I felt that merely seeing them jogging round the ship would have been rather boring. I managed to inject additional merriment by involving the deck games, the cafeteria, the shops, running up and down the stairs in the ballroom, running across in front of the screen in the crowded cinema, suspecting that it was Onslow behind a newspaper in one of the lounges when it was, in fact, Lord Lichfield – who happened to be on board when we were filming and who very sportingly agreed to my request to become involved.

His Lordship was actually on board as a guest lecturer (on photography, of course) and, having chatted to him whilst we were setting up the sequence – including, of course, giving him details of the short dialogue between Patricia, Clive and himself (which I had written the night before) – I realised that he was on board unaccompanied. That evening I rang him in his cabin and asked whether he would like to join myself, Patricia, Clive, Geoffrey, Judy and Eric Flounders (the Cunard public-relations officer) for dinner. He said he would love to and, in fact, joined us on two consecutive evenings. He was great fun and very sociable.

Incidentally, at breakfast in the hotel where we were staying in Southampton, on the morning that we were due to go on board the *QE2*, one of my team drew my attention to a newspaper article announcing the names of the recipients on the next Honours List – which included Patricia being awarded an OBE. We congratulated her and, understandably, she was obviously very thrilled that people now knew what, until then, had been a secret. I have often wondered whether the reason she was given the honour had anything to do with the fact that the Queen Mother was a huge fan of *Keeping Up Appearances*.

In fact, when I had originally discovered the previous year that Her Majesty liked the series so much, I began to send her videos of the various episodes, which her private secretary used to acknowledge, confirming the pleasure the Queen Mother obtained from watching them.

Anyway, back to the script! In the original version, despite seeing Onslow and Daisy at the Captain's cocktail party, and, later, watching them being welcomed by the Captain at his table in the first-class dining room, Hyacinth still thinks they are stowaways and the episode ended with her waiting on deck to try and talk to them. When they don't appear she decides to look into the lifeboat which she had previously seen Onslow coming down from (as part of their tour round the ship) and, as a result, she and Richard are arrested as stowaways.

A nice twist but it meant that we never saw Hyacinth's reaction to discovering, much to her chagrin, that Onslow and Daisy aren't stowaways but first-class 'honoured' passengers. This seemed to me to be a great shame and I was convinced that the audience would want to see her reaction to this staggering piece of news. Also, of course, the theory that Hyacinth and Richard were stowaways would hardly have stood up – even if Hyacinth had to reluctantly admit their surname was Bucket – because all they would have needed to do was show their tickets and cabin key and thus prove that they were legitimate passengers.

As fans of the series will probably remember my version was somewhat different. I wrote a scene in Hyacinth's cabin in which we see Richard return from having researched Onslow and Daisy's presence on the ship, tell his wife about the competition and describe the size of their cabin and their luxurious lifestyle on board to a horrified – and insanely jealous – Hyacinth whose nose is really put out!

I then wrote a scene in the Grand Lounge where we see her witnessing – with very bad grace – the cruise director introducing Onslow and Daisy to the other passengers as the winners of the competition. Finally, I showed Hyacinth swallowing her pride and dancing with Onslow in order that some of his glory might rub off onto her.

The dancing situation was interesting because Judy has since told me that, just before we were due to film that element, Patricia had been worried because she had just discovered that neither Clive nor Geoffrey could dance! Judy told me that she suggested that Pat just moved her arms to the music and that way their two partners would get away with it. In the event this worked. Mind you, it was just as well that I had arranged with the MD that the music would change to a very up-tempo number during which Hyacinth and Onslow let their hair down. If it had been something more precise – like a waltz – I don't think we *would* have got away with it!

In all, apart from the usual 'alterations' – there was an additional seventeen minutes written by myself – the episode was very successful. Roy never said a thing. Christopher subsequently told him that I wasn't able to film Hyacinth waiting for Onslow and Daisy on deck because it was very rough that night so I had written the last four-minute scene – the one set in the Grand Lounge – that evening. In reality, the script for that scene (and the previous one set in their cabin) had been locked in a cupboard in my office for six weeks before we had gone filming!

By the way, our filming with the *QE2* involved two sessions. On the first occasion we did all the scenes in the departure lounge and on the dockside with the ship leaving in the background and, on the second occasion, we were on board when she left Southampton. The two sessions were necessary for very good reasons. First, unlike Hyacinth, we didn't expect the ship to come back for us once we'd filmed the dockside material and, secondly, Pat is not that strong a swimmer!

There are some other things about the filming of that episode that you may find interesting. For instance, although we knew that Prince Edward was going to be on board when the ship left Southampton – as part of the celebrations of the fortieth anniversary of the coronation of Her Majesty the Queen – I hadn't realised that this would mean that the plans we had made to film three short scenes immediately after we had set sail would have to be scuppered – to use seagoing terminology.

Incidentally, when I had discovered a few weeks earlier that Prince Edward was going to be on board I had asked him if he would consider playing the role eventually taken on by Lord Lichfield, but he declined my offer!

As a result of the Prince being on board, there were several different cocktail parties to mark the presence of His Royal Highness and I didn't really feel that I could stop the artistes and members of my crew from attending their particular function. The event to which Patricia was invited was obviously the key one and I saw her sitting alongside Prince Edward chatting. I know she was a little embarrassed because she was already dressed and made up for the filming we were going to be doing as soon as the functions were over and, as she told me afterwards, she hoped that the Prince didn't think that she always wore such a glamorous hat! (Hyacinth's hats, by the way, were made by the same milliner that made the Queen Mother's.)

Because of the need for her hair to look immaculate for the filming, Pat was excused from wearing her life jacket during the obligatory boat drill that all passengers have to attend. His Royal Highness departed by helicopter once the ship had gone down Southampton Water and I was able to get on with some of the filming. I should point out that I have always been very correct when it comes to employing professional background artists ('extras' as they are usually known) ensuring they come through reputable agencies and are members of Equity. However, there will sometimes be occasions when, however much you want to be loyal and stick strictly to the rules, this really isn't possible for practical reasons.

Our filming on board the *QE2* was a prime example as there was obviously no way that I could take extras on board with us because accommodating them would have taken up valuable cabin space which, understandably, wouldn't have gone down very well with Cunard. Besides, just how many extras would I have needed, for example, to populate the dining room, the ballroom, the cinema – to say nothing of the actual decks!

Apart from the regulars involved, the only other actors I took on board were those required to play specific roles – namely the restaurant manager and the officer who shows Onslow and Daisy round the ship.

During the cruise the passengers were extremely helpful and I had encouraged them to be so by having copies of the following letter left in every cabin and outside the purser's office.

## KEEPING UP APPEARANCES

## FILMING FOR THE ABOVE COMEDY SERIES ON BOARD THE *QE2*

As I believe you know, I shall be recording some sequences for a special episode (which will be shown at Christmas) on this cruise. We will be most careful not to interfere with your life on board but I would be most grateful if you, for your part, would be kind enough to help us. We will be filming in various areas during the next few days and you may very easily come across us doing so.

May I ask you to please behave like perfectly normal passengers – do not stop and stare at the camera or the actors and do not point us out to your friends and relatives – or wave! You would be amazed at the number of times this happens when we are filming in public places.

If you're with someone who hasn't noticed us, warn them not to turn around and *then* tell them that they may well be on television at Christmas. If you are passing, try and walk as quietly as possible (normally but quietly) – it's amazing how much noise is created by clacking heels.

Whilst I am generally asking you *not* to look at the actors, there will be times when Hyacinth and Richard (especially the former) are behaving oddly. If you realise that the action would invite attention then, by all means, watch what they are up to as they pass you or you pass them – in fact, it would look odd if you didn't. But, please, don't come back for a second look!

Finally, there will be times when we shall have a requirement for 'extras'. If you are over, say, thirty-five and especially if you admit to being around fifty to fifty-five, we might well be able to use you for an hour or so during the cruise. We certainly need people for a scene which is supposed to take place at the Captain's cocktail party and another scene in the Grand Lounge – for both of these we will need the ladies in cocktail dresses and the gentlemen in dinner suits.

If you would like to be involved please leave your name at the purser's office and a member of my team will contact you. Thank you for reading this and may I wish you a very pleasant cruise aboard this wonderful ship.

Harold Snoad, Producer/Director of 'Keeping Up Appearances'


The evening before the *QE2* was due to depart Peter and I, plus Eric Flounders, went on board and had a meeting with the very helpful captain (John Barton-Hall), who confirmed that everything we were planning to do – and when we planned to do it – fitted in with the general everyday plans for the ship and they were perfectly happy with our proposed schedule.

During the time we were filming, the *QE2* was on a Baltic cruise and myself, the artists and the various members of my crew were due to fly back from Oslo (which, for the purposes of our filming, masqueraded as Copenhagen) four days later.

On every cruise there is at least one night when the passengers don evening dress (dinner suits) and as our filming plans didn't – for various reasons – match up with the nights planned by Cunard, they very kindly changed things so that the 'evening dress' night coincided with the night I needed it.

Everything went very well with all the filming, the only hitch occurring with one of the sequences planned for the aforementioned 'evening dress' night. The three sequences in question – and in order

112

of filming – were Hyacinth seeing Onslow and Daisy at the Captain's cocktail party, then her subsequently seeing them at the Captain's table in the dining room and, finally, the scene in the ballroom.

The Captain joined us as planned and we filmed the cocktail party scene and then moved into the first-class dining room and set up our equipment there. However, three-quarters of an hour after the time he had agreed to rejoin us there was still no sign of the Captain and then one of his officers arrived and told me that, owing to the ship's position with regard to the Norwegian coast, the Captain would have to stay on the bridge and, regrettably, wouldn't be able to film with us as originally arranged.

Obviously this sort of thing happens and we had no alternative but to grab a quick snack – no time for a proper meal – and move on to the scene in the ballroom. This went very well, although I only needed to film the element that involved Onslow, Daisy, the dancers, the cruise director and the band, and Hyacinth joining Onslow on the dance floor, because, earlier that afternoon, I had pre-filmed the part where Hyacinth and Richard are sitting on the sidelines watching the events – helped by some passengers who had been kind enough to don their evening attire and be seen in the background.

A particularly good example of how cooperative the passengers and crew were was the way I managed to get out of the problem of not being able to film the dining room scene as planned. Because we would have left the ship by the following evening, I asked whether any passengers in the first-class dining room would be prepared to don their dinner suits at lunchtime the following day. A hundred and fifty people were kind enough to do so, plus the waiting staff, who wear a different attire for serving dinner as distinct from lunch. We closed the curtains and you would never have known it was daylight outside. It was particularly kind of the passengers who volunteered because we were also in port that day and they could have been looking round Oslo!

The passengers were also very helpful when I decided to have Hyacinth and Richard jogging past the cinema screen. This was a last-minute idea on my part but it only took one announcement over the Tannoy to get at least a hundred and fifty people to turn up fifteen minutes later. The cinema projectionist put on one of the films they were currently showing on that cruise but, for copyright reasons, Andy, my VT editor, had to subsequently matt this out and replace it with material we had previously shot for Onslow's telly.

The only scenes that weren't actually filmed on board were those set in Hyacinth and Richard's cabin. When the ship had been in port at Southampton on our earlier filming session (where Hyacinth misses the sailing) I had shown my designer – the very clever Derek Evans – a typical cabin and he produced an excellent reconstruction in the studio. The reason I did this was because there were quite a few of these scenes and, therefore, they would have taken a long time to film on board and also, although the real cabins certainly aren't small, we would have been very short of space with the addition of technical equipment, lights and so on. It would also, of course, taken much longer to film the scenes with one camera rather than record them in the studio with five.

It also meant, of course, that the studio audience were present when these scenes were recorded whereas, had I shot them on the actual ship, they would have had considerably less 'live' action to watch in the studio.

I touched earlier on Clive Swift's reluctance, on a few occasions, to take direction. An amusing example of this was in one of those cabin scenes. There was a point in the story when Richard was obviously getting very browned off by the fact that Hyacinth kept changing her outfit – convinced that what she had previously chosen wasn't, for some reason, quite right. The script called for her to come out of the bathroom where she had been changing into yet another dress and say to Richard, 'What do you think?' At this point Richard – who was supposed to he paying no attention and looking in totally the opposite direction – said, 'I like it.' Whereupon Hyacinth responded by saying, 'You haven't even looked at it!'

As they were supposedly on a liner, at sea at the time, I plotted things so that Richard had his back to her and was concentrating on looking out of the porthole as he spoke to Hyacinth. Clive, however, didn't like this idea and wanted to be not only facing her but looking at her as he said his line, which, of course, made a total nonsense of Hyacinth's reply as I tactfully pointed out to him – as did Patricia.

At rehearsals the next day I suggested that, if he didn't want to

114

look out of the porthole, he could be engrossed in reading some of the *QE2* literature that was on the dressing table unit in front of the porthole. That way he would still have his back to Hyacinth as he said, 'I like it.' However, he was reluctant to accept this idea either and continued to want to look at Hyacinth as he said the line.

Finally, he came up with the suggestion that he could be on the other side of the panelling between the cabin 'hall' and the main room and for that reason he wasn't able to see Hyacinth when he said the line. For the sake of a quiet life I reluctantly agreed, but I still think my original suggestion was better, especially as Hyacinth's reply was geared to the fact that he had chosen not to look at what she was wearing rather than her being round the corner and, therefore, out of his sight. Mind you, I never regretted for one moment giving him the part of Richard because he was wonderful and brought so much to it.

The BBC's Publicity Department sends the press VHS copies of shows prior to them being transmitted to assist them with their previews. When they sent out the *QE2* episode I made quite sure that a Photostat copy of a note from myself accompanied each one asking them to be very careful not to publicise the fact in advance of transmission that Onslow and Daisy had won the competition and were on board the *QE2* unbeknown to Hyacinth.

I felt it was very important that the viewer didn't know this in advance; otherwise it was a bit like watching a whodunit already armed with the knowledge that the butler had done it! Fortunately, the newspapers all obliged and the story wasn't leaked. I also had to ensure that the BBC's Presentation Department didn't put out any 'trails' that gave the game away.

The episode was extremely well received by the viewers – and Cunard were also very happy with the end result.

# Another Christmas Special

As it was not going to be possible to make a series in 1994 because Patricia was heavily tied up with other things – mainly at the Festival Theatre, Chichester – it was decided that we would make a one-off 'special' for showing the following Christmas. Because of Pat's limited availability, this would have to be made in February – the earliest I had ever made a Christmas Special!

Around this time there was a change made to the Head of Entertainment. Jimmy Moir moved sideways and became Controller of Radio 2 and David Liddiment came from ITV to take over Jimmy's role. Each producer had a chat with him and, when it was my turn, I put him fully in the picture regarding the problems we had experienced over the past three years with the original versions of a lot of the scripts and explained that, because Roy sadly refused to listen to our views and seldom even considered doing any re-writes, we'd been forced into a position where there had been no other alternative but for me to come to the rescue. He appeared to be very interested and made no adverse comment.

I also had a meeting with Alan Yentob (the then Controller of BBC1) about various projects and, in the course of our conversation, I said that, although it was going to be quite difficult to top the *QE2* Christmas special, I had an idea that might be useful. I explained that I had a contact at Disney World in Florida who was madly keen on *Keeping Up Appearances* and would love us to film an episode there.

I told Alan that I had mentioned the idea to Patricia when she and I had a meal together a few evenings earlier and she had thought it was wonderful. Alan asked me to discuss it with David Liddiment. I did so and gave him my idea for how it might work:

117

## Suggestion for a *Keeping Up Appearances* special

Hyacinth receives a letter from a distant relative who now lives in America. He has obviously done well for himself – perhaps he sends a picture of his home – and he apparently holds an important position on the board of some large organisation, although he doesn't say which!

He is now in his sixties and has decided to spend some of his money on inviting certain members of his family to America (all expenses paid) for a short holiday and a special do to celebrate his fortieth wedding anniversary (or some similar function). The letter is to invite Hyacinth and Richard.

Hyacinth is elated but a few minutes later her enthusiasm is a little 'dampened' by a phone call from Daisy to say that she and Onslow – and Rose – have also had a letter!

We see the five of them go off by plane – possible filming on board with Hyacinth very put out that her down-market relatives are with her in the first-class section of the plane – and a car meets them at Orlando Airport and takes them to a smart hotel. It is night and there is a message at reception from their host saying that he apologises for having to accommodate them in this particular hotel but, unfortunately, there weren't any vacancies at the one he had intended to use.

As Hyacinth thinks the hotel they are in is excellent, she wonders just how good the other one would have been! The message goes on to say that their host will send a car for them in the morning to take them to his place of work where – after being shown around – they will be able to have lunch together.

In the morning a stretch limo arrives and whisks the five of them away. It stops outside the entrance to a large concern and it is only as Hyacinth gets out of the car and their host steps forward to welcome them – accompanied by Mickey and Minnie Mouse – that she realises that they are at Disney World and learns that the distant relative holds a responsible position within that organisation.

Onslow, Daisy and Rose are thrilled and really looking forward to the rest of the day. Hyacinth, being Hyacinth, is appalled.

What on earth is she doing at such a place? Thank goodness nobody she knows will see her. The others eagerly get involved in what is on offer – including Richard, much to Hyacinth's horror – and, of course, Hyacinth gradually capitulates.

We would, of course, need a suitable subplot to 'thicken' the episode and it will need a good tag, but I am working on that. I realise that there could be some concern about 'product placement' but, to be honest, Disney is the renowned leader of this sort of thing and, rather like the *QE2*, Rolls Royce and *The Times*, is sufficiently well known anyway. There's only really one of each in the top league and, in the world of theme parks, it's Disney.

It is not as if we would be singling out Chessington World of Adventures, Thorpe Park or Alton Towers for a 'mention', which it could reasonably be argued would be providing an advert for that one organisation.

The idea was turned down because it smacked of 'product placement'. This seemed particularly ironic when a few weeks later an episode of another sitcom, *Next of Kin*, went filming at one of the three mentioned above (I won't tell you which because that could be regarded as 'product placement'!) and, in the process, blatantly advertised that one over and above its competitors!

Instead, we just waited for Roy's script for this episode.

## CHRISTMAS SPECIAL 1994

**Plot:** Hyacinth is interested in getting new worktops in her kitchen whilst Richard has a fungal problem with his foot, which Hyacinth wants to disguise as something more acceptable. Over at Daisy and Onslow's Rose discovers that there's someone else in Daddy's bed.

**Cast:** Hyacinth (*Patricia Routledge*); Richard (*Clive Swift*); Liz (*Josephine Tewson*); Daisy (*Judy Cornwell*); Onslow (*Geoffrey Hughes*); Rose (*Mary Millar*); Emmet (*David Griffin*); Vicar (*Jeremy*

*Gittins*); Salesman (*Trevor Bannister*); Customer (*Andrew Bicknell*); His Wife (*Caroline Strong*); Mr Mawsby (*Preston Lockwood*); Daddy (*George Webb*)

**Additional locations:** Kitchen shop (In-Toto Kitchens, Leamington Spa)

When the original script arrived for this 'special' there were a number of things that Christopher and I didn't like, others that we didn't think worked, and elements that we (and Patricia) felt were basically weak. Overall, we felt that the episode was very ordinary and there was certainly nothing 'special' about it. Although, surprisingly, Martin Fisher didn't seem to think it was quite as bad as we did, he agreed that there was very little point in going back to our writer regarding our many reservations, because, of course, we all knew from past experience, that it was extremely unlikely that he would agree to make any alterations. A particularly difficult situation in view of the fact that Christopher and myself both felt there was an awful lot that needed changing. Martin left me with the words 'See what you can do with it.'

Having read it several times I came to the conclusion that, for a start, more could be made of the fact that Hyacinth was planning a new kitchen. In the original version she had asked the Vicar round to seek his guidance on whether the name of a certain worktop colour ('Passion Flame') would be compatible with her remaining a member of his congregation but, after that, the business of her wanting a new kitchen had been completely dropped, which, I thought, was a pity.

I wrote a whole scene in a kitchen shop in which she is distinctly put out at hearing a young couple discussing with the salesman the posh kitchen they are planning and then her being extremely disappointed to learn that the worktop colour she is now interested in, 'Angel Gabriel Blue', is no longer available – mainly because she has been looking at last year's brochure! She bullies the assistant into ringing the manufacturers to see if they could possibly find her some and, whilst he is on the phone, sets about testing the surface of another worktop made by the same manufacturer – with various substances – as the salesman discovers, to his horror, on his return.

Patricia waiting for last minute adjustments to the camera before climbing the wall – or appearing to do so!

Harold with Patricia fooling around after she returns with her clothes in tatters following her encounter with the randy Major.

Directing the scene in which Hyacinth gets involved in Church cleaning duties.

Filming on the river with me reading for Patricia.

Patricia about to go horse riding – on the camera dolly!

Harold and Patricia with the bull used in a scene in this episode.

(Xmas 93) Patricia, Lord Lichfield and Harold having just had dinner together on the *QE2* after filming.

Suggesting some comedy business to Clive on location.

Harold with Mary – especially taken
for the scene in which she and
Daisy are sorting through photos
of Rose with her ex-fiancés.

Harold with Rose, Daisy and Onslow whilst filming at Walton Hall.

David Griffin, Josephine Tewson, myself and Patricia on location during a break in filming.

Patricia drying my hair after coming off the log flume at Great Yarmouth.

Fooling around with Patricia during a rehearsal break in the studio.

Harold directing a scene outside Onslow and Daisy's (Clive isn't bored – just tired!)

Mary, myself and Judy after lunch at our home.

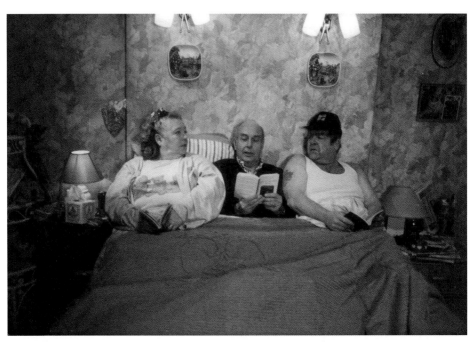

An 'off duty' moment. In bed with Daisy and Onslow during filming for 'Memoirs' for American TV.

I then wrote a new bedroom scene for Daisy, Onslow and Rose; extra material for the start of a scene in Hyacinth's kitchen with Liz and Emmet; a second kitchen scene in which Hyacinth produces a pink plastic baby cup for Elizabeth – to avoid further breakages – and then gets Emmet to Sellotape the lid on, only for Liz to subsequently find, of course, that she can't put any sugar in; and a further scene in which Elizabeth, on hearing Hyacinth's phone ring, accidentally nudges Emmet and makes him spill his coffee.

In the original version Roy had Hyacinth making Richard wear a very bulky bandage on his foot to give the impression that his problem was 'up-market' gout and not 'down-market' fungus. A funny idea, but he had also said that Richard would drive the car wearing this. I honestly didn't believe that Richard would agree to do this, as it would obviously have been extremely dangerous. I re-wrote it so that, once he was in the car, he slid the huge bandage off expecting to slip into a spare pair of shoes that he thought were in the rear of the car. When Hyacinth tells him they're in the hall cupboard he wants to go back inside for them but she insists that they haven't got time and he'd better drive barefoot. After all, people in Nigeria often drive with bare feet! This worked very well – the results were just as funny but rather more believable.

In my version when they arrive at Onslow's, Hyacinth finds Rose having an amorous goodbye kiss with a boyfriend who just happens to be the kitchen salesman – much to his and Hyacinth's embarrassment.

I then wrote another scene which pursued the worktop story in which we see Daisy take Hyacinth into her kitchen and proudly show her a length of worktop which Onslow is going to install. She tells Hyacinth that they were giving away off-cuts of it down the tip. Hyacinth immediately recognises it as the Angel Gabriel Blue she has just ordered and the thought of her having the same worktop as Onslow makes her feel quite ill!

While they are there Richard is coerced into climbing a ladder to have a look through the window of a bedroom where there is an unknown man sleeping in Daddy's bed.

In the original version the final scene started with Daddy arriving back on his skateboard and looking surprised at seeing Richard hanging upside down with his bandaged foot caught in the ladder. However, we never saw how Richard came to finish up like that, which I found quite amazing. The previous scene had ended with Hyacinth saying that she couldn't climb the ladder and Daisy saying she wouldn't let Onslow do it, but that was it.

I wrote a different scene in which we see Richard being encouraged to climb upwards, *then* Daddy returning and a series of events happening as Daisy, Onslow, Rose and Hyacinth go to greet him at the gate – including Onslow being accidentally knocked backwards over the hedge by Hyacinth. Add the dog's sudden barking to Onslow's yell and there was very good reason for Richard to slip off the ladder.

Incidentally, the wider shot of Daddy skateboarding was achieved by using a stand-in. In the closer shot, it is Daddy; however, he is not actually on a skateboard but is making the right body movements as he is pulled along on the camera dolly.

As well as re-writing quite a lot of the original I added over twenty minutes of new material written by myself and the studio audience loved it. So did the viewing public, as was subsequently proved by their reaction to the episode.

There is a scale of viewer appreciation for television programmes called the A.I. (Appreciation Index). This has nothing to do with the number of people watching – which in the case of *Keeping Up Appearances* was always very high – but is a measure of how much a sample viewer audience (approximately five thousand people) enjoyed a show on a scale of 1 to 100. A good situation comedy generally comes out at about 78 to 82. If it was in the 50s or early 60s you definitely had a flop on your hands!

The A.I. for episodes of *Keeping Up Appearances* was always very good – generally in the 80s – but it is interesting that it was six points higher for this episode on which I had done so much re-writing than for the episode I was going to make for Christmas 1995 which I altered very little for reasons that will became clear later on.

Six months before it was due to be transmitted, I put David Liddiment fully in the picture regarding what I had done to achieve the Christmas Special and left him with a copy of the script with everything I had written highlighted. He thanked me and appeared to be somewhat in awe that I had been able to come to the rescue in the way that I had. I also gave Martin a VHS of the end result.

The rest of my year was taken up doing a totally different project, but the dates for a fifth series to be made in 1995 had all been arranged. Around this time someone from the BBC's Drama Department went to Alan Yentob with an idea for using Patricia in a series revolving around a North Country 'housewife' who becomes a private detective. Presumably they felt that, because Patricia was now so popular with the fans of *Keeping Up Appearances*, this would be an asset on a new project from the point of view of attracting viewers. She was also, of course, right for the part.

Alan Yentob immediately agreed but it was perhaps rather unfortunate that he did so without any consultation with myself because I knew Pat well enough to know that she would find the idea of playing a new character very tempting and her loyalty to *Keeping Up Appearances* would be threatened. Sadly, this certainly became the case and, had she not already signed a contract to do the fifth series, I'm not at all sure the show wouldn't have finished there and then!

Christmas came and the 'special' proved to be very popular with the viewers. There appeared to be no adverse reaction from our writer, which I was obviously very pleased about. However, ten days later the bomb fell – or the ship finally hit the iceberg! I was called into Martin Fisher's office and told that Roy had apparently recorded the special, watched it ten days after Christmas and that he had subsequently written to David Liddiment complaining that I had tampered with his original.

The content of his letter must have been pretty strong because, as a result, both David and Martin went up to Doncaster (a distance of some two hundred miles) the following day to see him. I was *never* allowed to see the letter (which was extremely unfair) but I have since discovered from a reliable source that it said something along the lines of him stating that he would never write anything for the BBC again. This would certainly have accounted for the way the hierarchy panicked.

When David and Martin got back, David called me in to see him and tore me apart limb from limb. He made no mention of the fact that I had already told him what I had done to the episode and why it had been necessary, nor to the fact that I had also given him a copy of my re-written version. Instead, he just shouted at me telling me that I should never have altered a word of the original and that under no circumstances should I interfere with any of the scripts for the fifth series. If there was an Oscar category for 'Best bad-tempered performance' he would definitely have won it! He said it didn't matter if the scripts for the next series were 'blatantly repetitive, totally illogical or unfunny'!

As I'm sure you can imagine, I walked out of his office feeling somewhat shattered. During this extremely bad-tempered tirade Martin Fisher – the person who had asked me to do what I could with the original script for the 'special' and who had thoroughly approved of the end result – just sat there without saying a word!

Mind you, I had noticed at least a year earlier that, although Martin totally agreed with me about the problems with a number of the original scripts, he was always very reluctant to give me any form of official backing. He and I would discuss the things that Christopher and I weren't happy about and Martin would then go up to see our writer to pass on the various problems. Actually 'pass' is very appropriate terminology because when he returned it was obvious that he'd failed to mention quite a few of the things we had listed.

Incidentally, a couple weeks after that dreadful meeting I sent David Liddiment a note saying that I was somewhat shattered by his reaction to Roy's letter and the way he had told me off so brutally. He responded with a note saying that the bottom line was that there had been a breakdown in communication between myself and Roy Clarke and that he had to protect the BBC's position as he saw fit.

A breakdown in communication there may have been but it wasn't for want of trying on my part.

# The Last Series and a Final Christmas Special

When Roy Clarke had been commissioned to write the fifth series –
at least four months before the transmission of the Christmas episode
– I had sent him a polite note:

*'Just a few points worth mentioning: 1) During the last series we
had several letters from viewers (and one was published in a national
newspaper) pointing out that Richard's car is still a D-reg model
and rather surprised that Hyacinth would tolerate this.*

*Obviously, I could merely change the car for something more up
to date but it seems a pity to do this if you could build an episode
around Hyacinth realising that their car is doing nothing for her
image and telling Richard that they must upgrade it to something
better.*

*In case it slips your mind, Hyacinth and Richard still have their
bijou but extremely cramped flat in the converted ex-stately home
in the country. Whilst I wouldn't want to do too much of the series
involving this property (or too much location work there because it
is open to the public and consequently our hours of filming would
be somewhat limited), it seems a pity not to use it at least once.*

*I was wondering if there was anything in either of these two
ideas:*

*a) Hyacinth hears that the chairperson of the residents' committee
is moving on and volunteers herself for the job – much to the horror
of the other residents on the committee. She could try and bring in
a lot of new draconian regulations – virtually all of which would
be broken when Onslow et al. visit.*

*b) Hyacinth decides that she doesn't like the country way of life
as much as she had originally envisaged and hits upon the idea of
letting the flat out for a couple of weeks here and there – but, of*

125

*course, she has to personally vet the people answering her advert to*
*see if they are the right class and, once they are in, continually*
*check up on whether they are obeying the 'house rules' she has laid*
*down.*
    *Regards,*
    *Harold'*

Once again I received no response.

At the time the aforementioned 'explosion' occurred we had already received Episodes 1 to 6 of Series 5 and, unfortunately, there was very little that could be described as either strong or different in the way of storylines. Martin agreed with me that the six scripts were, on the whole, pretty poor and was also aware that I had already re-written – with his agreement – large elements of the first four.

During David Liddiment's tirade he had also said that, in the past, I shouldn't have shown Patricia the original scripts. A rather odd statement in the circumstances. What was the point of sending copies of the original scripts to Patricia and the other members of the cast a couple of weeks before the start of the location work (as is the usual timescale) knowing that a lot of work needed to be done on them? What was very interesting about David's comment was that, in an indirect way, he was more or less saying that the reason I shouldn't let Patricia see the original versions when they first arrived was because they weren't strong enough!

It was just as well I had sent them to Patricia because when she saw the original scripts for this series she was hardly over the moon – which rather proved that I was right to be concerned about the content! Incidentally, Christopher Bond had only stayed around for the arrival of the first two episodes of this series. He had then told me that he couldn't carry on any longer because having to talk to our writer was proving too stressful. I was very sorry to see him go because he provided me with a very useful second opinion regarding the original versions.

Martin went up to see our writer (who, as usual, wasn't prepared to talk to me about the scripts and was supposed to discuss with him various observations regarding Episodes 5 and 6 but he returned having, once again, only discussed very few of the long list of things which he and I had agreed needed to be raised. What he did do was to leave Roy with copies of my versions of Episodes 1 to 4. A few days later these were sent back to me with everything that I had penned scored through and some nasty comments added. Incidentally, although Patricia had been appalled by the original scripts of these four, she had been delighted with my re-written versions.

The last four episodes started to arrive and they only confirmed my feelings that, overall, these ten episodes were very weak. As I had been told by David Liddiment not to meddle with them, obviously something drastic had to be done in order for us to finish up with a series which would be to a standard acceptable by the viewer – and worthy of the BBC.

Roy agreed to see Martin and myself – the only script conference we ever had in five years – and we went up to Doncaster. I suspect that David Liddiment may have suggested that he ought to see us but I have no proof of this. Roy met us at the station and drove us to a local Travel Inn-type establishment which had a small conference room we could use for our meeting. I started by very politely handing him a list of reasons why I had made alterations to Episodes 1 to 4 – which Martin was supposed to have given him on his earlier trip but had obviously not done so.

I then tactfully tried to raise the various points which Martin and I had agreed needed addressing regarding the other six episodes, but our writer, who was, shall we say, not in a particularly receptive mood, declined to discuss any of them. In fact, on a couple of occasions he got up and thumped the wall. Martin sat at the end of the table and didn't utter one single word in two hours!

Eventually, because I realised that we weren't getting anywhere (and I was concerned that the BBC might have to pick up the bill for any cracks in the walls!), I suggested that we call it a day – the one point with which Roy agreed! However, I did tell him as tactfully as possible that Martin and I had jointly decided that an episode about Rose getting married wasn't going to be made because we thought it just didn't work.

I very politely pointed out that we had two alternatives. We would either have to make only nine episodes instead of ten or he would need to write a replacement episode. At this point I handed him a possible storyline, tactfully saying that I wasn't suggesting that he had to use it but it might prove useful. At first he wouldn't even pick it up off the table but, eventually, when I said that if he didn't like it he could just put it in the wastepaper basket, he did take it – albeit extremely grudgingly.

I then suggested that, although the meeting hadn't been that fruitful, we might as well finish off by having a drink together. Roy agreed and he and I went off to the bar, but Martin said that he had to go to reception to pay for the conference room. Roy and I chatted perfectly reasonably over our drinks talking about normal everyday things and kept off the subject of *Keeping Up Appearances*.

Martin finally joined us having taken thirty-five minutes to pay the bill! I remember wondering if he had been deliberately keeping out of the way because he thought Roy and I might be arguing – which wasn't the case. A few days later Roy sent me a script for an episode based on the storyline I had left with him – namely, the one where Richard forgets their wedding anniversary and, in a panic, arranges to have a burglar alarm system fitted as a supposedly surprise anniversary present. Unfortunately, when he subsequently lets himself in he can't remember the security code and the alarm goes off – the code which Hyacinth chose to give the installers being the date of their wedding!

I rang Roy to thank him for the script and commented that I thought it worked very well. He thanked me for the compliment but, strangely, didn't thank me for the basic idea! After I had re-written two of the scenes, this episode gained the highest appreciation figure of the ten episodes making up the series, which was rather gratifying. It was also later chosen as a video release in the States.

The following day Roy sent me copies he had obviously made of my re-written versions of the first four scripts we had received – the ones that Martin had given him and which Roy had subsequently returned – with a large amount of my material that he had originally scored out, reinstated!

Because time was marching on and I hadn't really got any-where with the elements of the other five scripts that I had tried to discuss when we were up at Doncaster, I rang Roy again and politely enquired what he wanted to do about the re-writes for these. His reply (said very pleasantly) was 'Oh, you do whatever you think is necessary.' I therefore re-wrote large elements of the remaining episodes – just as I had always done! And this was after he had strongly complained – in a manner that he knew would have worried the powers-that-be and would quite likely get me into trouble – about my re-writing his material for the Christmas Special! A little difficult to understand.

In fairness, he did agree to make a few minor alterations here and there.

Let's take a look at same of the problem areas of the original scripts for the fifth series and the solutions that I came up with. Remember that, in addition to these, I had to do umpteen re-writes – some of them whole scenes – in order to make sense of various elements of the dialogue or plots.

A good deal of this was after Patricia and I had discussed the various problems together during lengthy telephone conversations. Whilst she sometimes came up with a few suggestions, on the whole she would express her grave reservations regarding a certain element of a script and it would be left to me to put it right.

## EPISODE 1

**Plot:** Hyacinth volunteers her services to the Vicar to assist with a day's outing to the coast for pensioners but has her work cut out trying to avoid the romantic moves of Mr Farrini. The Onslow crowd has problems when Daddy goes missing.

**Cast:** Hyacinth (*Patricia Routledge*); Richard (*Clive Swift*); Liz (*Josephine Tewson*); Daisy (*Judy Cornwell*); Onslow (*Geoffrey Hughes*); Rose (*Mary Millar*); Emmet (*David Griffin*); Vicar (*Jeremy Gittins*); Vicar's Wife (*Marion Barron*); Mr Farrini (*Angus Lennie*); Mr Cooper-Bassett (*Derek Waring*); Mrs Lomax (*Rita Davies*); Police Sergeant (*Eric Carte*); Inspector (*John Darrell*); Lady Helper (*Sheila Rennie*)

**Additional locations:** Pleasure Beach Funfair (at Great Yarmouth)

There were a number of problems with this episode. Let's start with a small one. In the original version the Vicar asked his wife to go back inside the church hall to fetch a stool for him to stand on in order that he could pin the poster about the pensioners' outing on the notice board. This was to provide time to see Hyacinth and Richard passing the church hall in their car. Fair enough, but why on earth involve a stool? The Vicar is tall (6 feet 2) and if he was going to stand on a stool to put the poster up just how high was it going to be and – at that height what chance would anyone (least of all a pensioner with poor eyesight!) have of reading it? Hyacinth also needed to read it later when talking to the Vicar and it would have been about three feet above her head. I changed it to the Vicar's wife having forgotten the drawing pins. Unfortunately, this was another example of even the most basic logic apparently being totally unimportant to Roy.

There was a perfect example of this in an episode of Roy's series *Last of the Summer Wine*. One of the characters, Foggy, is asked by a friend, Howard, to deliver a note to Marina, a lady with whom Howard is having a long-standing fling. She works as a cashier at the local supermarket. When Foggy pays for his shopping he hands over the note to Marina. The note says 'Meet me at four o'clock at the bridge.' It has not been signed by Howard and as Foggy leaves the shop he realises from Marina's reaction to the note that she thinks it's from him.

Roy had Foggy panicking and spending the rest of the episode going through the most elaborate plans to try and find someone else to stand in for him at four o'clock – although it was perfectly obvious that there was absolutely no reason for him to be concerned because, when Marina turned up, Howard would be there waiting for her.

During the meeting Martin and I had with Roy in Doncaster I jokingly touched on the lack of logic in this plot but, although I suspect Roy knew that I was right, he certainly wasn't going to admit it.

Anyway, back to the pensioners' outing. Although Elizabeth arrived at the church hall with Hyacinth and Richard on the big day I think our writer then forgot that she was with them. There were seven pages during which she never uttered a single word. I changed that.

In the original version, when the minibus stops because Mrs Lomax was feeling ill, Hyacinth and Mr Farrini get off too – Mr Farrini chasing her – without either Richard or Liz noticing, which seemed somewhat unlikely. I changed this so that we see them aware of Hyacinth running out from behind the bus and added her line to Mr Farrini who is in hot pursuit of her: 'No, Mr Farrini, when I said I wanted to stretch my legs...', which got a big laugh and then to the original 'Do hurry, Mrs Lomax', I added: 'I think the country air is affecting Mr Farrini.'

When Hyacinth first saw the Cooper-Bassetts at the funfair in the original version she, rather surprisingly, totally accepted their presence there. In my version I wrote some extra dialogue between herself and Elizabeth which expressed her surprise at seeing them. I did this because, if the Cooper-Bassetts were so far upmarket – as Hyacinth is leading us to believe –would she really accept seeing them walking around a funfair and not make any comment. Although their presence there was explained later, I thought it would help if Hyacinth registered surprise when she first saw them.

When Peter and I visited the funfair during the recce for locations I spotted the Fun House and, having had a look round inside, I realised there was huge scope there (with the moving floors, the wind effect and the distorting mirrors), so I wrote the whole scene that involved Hyacinth, Mr Farrini and Mrs Lomax getting involved with those – and, of course, the scene before they go inside.

In the final version Mr Farrini and Hyacinth are together on the ghost train. In the original version it was supposed to be the tunnel of love. Apart from there being very few tunnels of love around these days – there certainly wasn't one at Yarmouth – I felt that a ghost train might be an advantage because, as well as having spooky things in front and to one side of her, Hyacinth could also have Mr Farrini scaring the life out of her with his romantic antics on the other side!

## EPISODE 2

**Plot:** Hyacinth is anxious to attend the mayor's fancy dress ball. However, as Richard has retired and is no longer a council employee, they are now not automatically on the guest list. Hyacinth sends her highly embarrassed husband to the town hall to make sure they receive an invitation. When she and Richard turn up on the night her nose is really put out when she discovers that the costume she has so carefully chosen is also being worn by others. Rose has a new boyfriend and Daisy reminisces about the days when she and Onslow were first together.

**Cast:** Hyacinth (*Patricia Routledge*); Richard (*Clive Swift*); Liz (*Josephine Tewson*); Daisy (*Judy Cornwell*); Onslow (*Geoffrey Hughes*); Rose (*Mary Millar*); Emmet (*David Griffin*); Postman (*David Janson*); Town Hall Official (*Ivor Danvers*); Mrs Donaghue (*Jean Harvey*); Boy (*Kyle Wicks*)

**Additional locations:** Int./ext. town hall (Leamington Spa); ext. Mrs Donaghue's (Greaves Close, Warwick)

There is a scene outside Hyacinth's where the postman bribes a small boy to put Hyacinth's mail through her letter box. In the original script there was no dialogue provided for this scene, which made it a little difficult to get it over. In retrospect, I wonder whether our writer sometimes used to forget what series he was writing. In *Last of the Summer Wine*, which was set in idyllic countryside, there were quite a few 'non-verbal' scenes with specially written mood music to back them. This was not the case with *Keeping Up Appearances*, which was a totally different type of show.

By the way, there was an amusing moment when I was filming this scene outside Hyacinth's – or should that be the Bouquet residence? In response to the boy asking for money for delivering the letter, the postman had to say '50p! You're going to grow up into a monster, aren't you?' At this point the boy stopped acting, turned to me and said, 'He makes me laugh.' In the final version Hyacinth goes to the mayor's fancy dress ball dressed as Boadicea and is extremely put out to discover that there are several other ladies there in identical costume – which was my idea.

In the original script Hyacinth isn't able to hire the costume she wants and therefore is supposed to have settled for wearing biker's gear. Whilst I fully realised that the sight of Hyacinth dressed as a motorcyclist would be a funny picture, I had to ask myself (and I'm sure a lot of the fans of the series would have had the same thought) whether Hyacinth – of all people – really would have gone to the mayor's ball dressed like that. Surely it was completely out of character for her to allow herself to be seen in something of that nature. It also seemed rather strange that although it was written that she is really embarrassed when Mrs Donaghue spots her in that costume, she is perfectly happy to turn up at the Mayor's ball wearing it!

Roy agreed to re-write this element but when he did so he changed Hyacinth's attire to that of a cowgirl! Once again, I felt that it was extremely unlikely that Hyacinth, with all her illusions of grandeur, would go to fancy dress ball dressed like that. Eventually Roy agreed to my Boadicea suggestion.

Incidentally, when Onslow's car turns up outside Mrs Donaghue's the original script said that the car already contained Onslow, Daisy, Rose and Mr Whatsit and yet Onslow was still able to give Hyacinth and Richard a lift to the town hall. I decided to leave Daisy out of the equation. By the way, if you look carefully at the scene when the car noisily backfires as it leaves the town hall, you will see an elderly man jump out of his skin. That was a real member of the public who, with others, was watching us filming.

This was another episode where I worked out a whole new routine for when Hyacinth invites Elizabeth in, yet again, for coffee. On this occasion I had Hyacinth telling Liz that she had arrived early (which she hadn't) because this allowed me to have Hyacinth continuing with her cake making and, thereby, obtain additional comedy from Liz being startled whilst drinking her coffee (a difficult enough process for her anyway in Hyacinth's house) by sudden loud noises as Hyacinth closes the oven door, throws a spoon into the mixing bowl and then noisily drops the latter into the sink. Later – whilst Hyacinth was on the telephone taking a call from Daisy – I had Elizabeth get rid of her coffee by pouring it down the sink, then decide to help herself from the biscuit tin only to be alarmed by Hyacinth's sudden reappearance and knock the whole tin onto the floor. I then had Hyacinth go back to the telephone with the line 'Onslow likes broken biscuits, doesn't he?' The sequence provided a lot of laughs.

# EPISODE 3

**Plot:** The burglar alarm episode I referred to earlier.

**Cast:** Hyacinth (*Patricia Routledge*); Richard (*Clive Swift*); Liz (*Josephine Tewson*); Daisy (*Judy Cornwell*); Onslow (*Geoffrey Hughes*); Rose (*Mary Millar*); Emmet (*David Griffin*); Vicar (*Jeremy Gittins*); Postman (*David Janson*); Security Representative (*Ian Lavender*); Engineers (*Graham Ibot, Ben De Winter*); Daddy (*George Webb*); Lady (*Margaret Towner*)

**Additional locations:** Pub where Richard and Emmet go for a drink (The Heathcote Inn, Leamington Spa)

There was an amusing moment during a scene in the kitchen when Hyacinth is showing the representative from the security firm round her property. He is engrossed in taking notes and working out the security arrangements for the bungalow when Hyacinth (who has requested an alarm which sounds like the *QE2*'s siren) had to suddenly say to the already highly stressed salesman 'I've sailed on her, you know.' As a result of this sudden interruption to his thoughts the salesman jumps and almost drops the file he is carrying. On the night he did this a little too strongly and the whole file shot in the air and landed on Pat – whereupon they both burst into hysterical laughter.

# EPISODE 4

**Plot:** Hyacinth makes plans for a 'waterside supper with riparian entertainment', which she thinks will be a step up from her normal candlelight suppers. She has chosen a specific part of the river bank for the event but is horrified when they turn up there on the day – along with Elizabeth, Emmet, the Vicar and his wife – to discover that it's now not quite as idyllic as when she first discovered it. They all take to the river instead with even more problems.

**Cast:** Hyacinth (*Patricia Routledge*); Richard (*Clive Swift*); Liz (*Josephine Tewson*); Daisy (*Judy Cornwell*); Onslow (*Geoffrey*

*Hughes*); Rose (*Mary Millar*); Emmet (*David Griffin*); Vicar (*Jeremy Gittins*); His Wife (*Marion Barron*); Postman (*David Janson*); Violet (*Anna Dawson*); Lock-keeper (*Steve Morley*); Daddy (*George Webb*)

**Additional locations:** River bank (near Shillingford); lock (Benson Lock)

This episode called for a huge amount to be shot on location. Although the original script included the very good scene between Hyacinth and the postman, the latter expresses absolutely no surprise when he learns that Hyacinth has sent an invitation to Liz and Emmet via the Royal Mail when – because they only live next door – any normal person would have just put it through their letter box. This certainly wasn't a huge point but I felt something could be made of it in the dialogue by the postman – and could be funny. I also believed that if the 'sane' people in Hyacinth's life didn't raise these points (on behalf of the viewer) they would *all* begin to look mad! Roy agreed to my suggestion.

In the scene between the Vicar and his wife the original script had the Vicar looking up Hyacinth's number in the local telephone book whereas surely an invitation – especially one sent by Hyacinth, who, let's face it, knows the right way to do these things – would have said RSVP and given them her number. When the Vicar rings Hyacinth, the directions said: 'The Vicar pulls the telephone away from his ear as torrents of conversation flow from Hyacinth. We can't hear what's she saying but we can hear that it's continuous.' In other words, it had to be loud enough to be heard but not understood.

I remember asking Martin Fisher if he thought Roy was going to object to my writing material for Hyacinth to say at the other end of the line (she needed to say *something*) or perhaps she could read an extract from *War and Peace*!

In the event I altered things so that we saw both ends of the conversation with the Vicar still not being able to get a word in edgeways. I hasten to add that in a number of cases – specifically calls from Sheridan, Violet, the Vicar and his wife, requests for Chinese meals, and so on – only seeing Hyacinth's end of the conversation

135

was certainly the best way. But this conversation was the other way round – we were at the Vicar's end of the phone.

At one point in this episode the script had Hyacinth talking on the telephone whilst, at the same time, closing the front door with her foot after the departing Elizabeth, whom she has hurriedly got rid of because she doesn't want her to hear what she is saying to Violet. Any fan of the series would have known that this would have been impossible unless Hyacinth had a leg measuring around eighteen feet! (or 5.48 metres if you've gone metric). I found it amazing that after thirty-six episodes Roy still didn't seem to know where the kitchen, telephone and front door were in relation to each other.

In the original version Hyacinth gets to her selected part of the river bank only to find the whole length completely occupied by fishermen – described as being 'shoulder to shoulder'. Where on earth was I supposed to obtain that number of fishermen? Moreover, as, strictly speaking, I would have to have used professional 'extras', this would have cost a bomb. I pointed out the impracticalities and our writer accepted my idea of the dredger, which, of course, as well as being noisy would bring up loads of smelly mud from the river bed. All in all, rather more off-putting if you're having a picnic than the presence of fishermen.

In the re-written version, the dredger becomes involved instead and we see Hyacinth and Richard getting totally drenched. However, in Roy's version of this, he had Hyacinth, who is sitting facing Richard (who, as the rower, is facing the stern of the boat), stand up on the pretence of looking ahead for a suitable picnic point. Nothing wrong with this except that she then sits down again – only this time next to Richard. There was no reason given for this – in fact it was completely contrary to the idea that she wanted to look ahead. It was purely so that, conveniently, they should both have their backs to the dredger they are approaching. I re-wrote this element so that she goes to help Richard with the rowing, thereby giving a reason for her move. I also came up with not only the idea of using the lock but also the tag for that scene. I also wrote the element outside Hyacinth's when she is too busy checking her lists to help Richard open the car door, the scene when she is leading the cars down the lane and the dialogue about closing the gate and the Vicar's response to this. Amongst *quite* a few other things!

## EPISODE 5

**Plot:** Hyacinth spots a pair of skis on the roof rack of an upmarket neighbour's car and this immediately gives her the idea of buying Richard a pair for his birthday. This will mean that they will be able to drive about with them on *their* roof rack and thereby impress other people. Unfortunately, they have to borrow Violet's roof rack and during the process of getting the skis over there things start to go pear-shaped – not helped by the fact Hyacinth insists on giving two ladies a lift which they don't need! She then discovers that Violet and Bruce's relationship has completely fallen apart. Rose also has men problems, which makes Daisy and Onslow consider their own day-to-day lives.

**Cast:** Hyacinth (*Patricia Routledge*); Richard (*Clive Swift*); Liz (*Josephine Tewson*); Daisy (*Judy Cornwell*); Onslow (*Geoffrey Hughes*); Rose (*Mary Millar*); Emmet (*David Griffin*); Vicar (*Jeremy Gittins*); Vicar's Wife (*Marion Barron*); Violet (*Anna Dawson*); Misses Pilsworth (*Lois Penson, Clare Kelly*); Bruce (*John Evitts*)

**Additional locations:** Ext. Violet's (Newbold Terrace East, Leamington Spa)

The original script for this episode didn't include any of the material about smuggling the skis into the property. It had only shown Hyacinth getting the idea of buying them and a couple of scenes later giving them to Richard as a birthday present.

I thought it was a little difficult to believe that since Scene 1 Hyacinth had been out and purchased a pair of skis, brought them home (she doesn't drive) or had them delivered (as Richard is retired he could well have been at home when they arrived), and then wrapped and hidden these very long objects in the bungalow without him being remotely aware. I pointed this out to Roy and his response was that I should 'insert shots of Hyacinth doing secretive things with the lengthy package'. In the event I made rather more of it than that and also added the appropriate dialogue.

I was also concerned that viewers were going to wonder – quite reasonably – why Richard takes the skis to Violet's to borrow her special roof rack when any normal person would collect the roof rack, bring it back and *then* put the skis on it. Whilst I obviously accepted that it was to allow the comedy business of the skis being too long to travel inside the car, I was a bit worried that viewers would be surprised that Richard didn't ask why they were taking the skis with them. I felt that, without him asking the sort of questions the viewer would ask, he was in grave danger of being seen as a complete idiot.

There is a scene in Hyacinth's drive in which we see Richard and Hyacinth having huge difficulties because of the limited space inside the car once they had loaded the skis. In the original version this scene didn't exist – we merely discovered them in the moving car on their way to Violet's, which I felt was a pity because there was obviously scope for comedy with such space-invading items.

In this episode a secondary theme revolved around Rose deciding that she would like to become a nun. We'd already done this in another episode, albeit with her having a different excuse – namely, getting to see the dishy Vicar. But it was still pretty well exactly the same thing.

When Hyacinth tells Richard to pull up because she has spotted the two Miss Pilsworths the original script said: 'We see Hyacinth scooping up the two old ladies despite their attempts to decline and bundle them into the back of the car'. The two ladies had no dialogue and our writer had presumably, once again, thought the action would be covered by 'mood' music. He also seemed to have forgotten that Hyacinth and Richard already had a large pair of skis on board which would occupy some of the back of the car as well as poke out of the front windows. Therefore, Hyacinth certainly wouldn't be able to get out in a hurry (as he had described) to intercept the ladies and would be unable to put them into the back of the car and replace the skis without quite a bit of trouble. I pointed this out and Roy did provide some dialogue to cover Hyacinth's attempts to fit them into the rear of the car before they eventually finish up sitting in the front with Hyacinth squashed in the back boxed in by the skis.

Incidentally, in the original version of the script, as well as having the two old ladies saying nothing when they are picked up, they also travel in the car totally mute. Whilst I certainly appreciated that Hyacinth would be doing all the talking, it was pretty obvious that they would surely try and interject – especially as they had almost been kidnapped! When I pointed this out to Roy he did agree to write same dialogue for them.

This was also yet another occasion – the fourth time in this series alone – where Hyacinth takes people round to Violet's in order to impress them and discovers Violet either tipsy or having a loud row with her husband. I honestly wondered whether it was believable – even in the world of comedy – that, in the light of her previous experiences, Hyacinth would be foolish enough to continue doing this and whether we could keep repeating the same joke. In the original version – after the two ladies have been witness to Violet's tantrums – Hyacinth gives instructions to Richard to reverse and tells the Misses Pilsworth that Richard will bring them back in a few moments. However, in the next scene at Violet's the script said: 'Richard's car is now parked without the two Miss Pilsworths.' As there was no mention of what had happened to them, I established that they were going to be put down at a bus stop and that they had originally been near their home – to which they were returning – when they were 'kidnapped'!

Towards the end of this episode Hyacinth and Richard are taking Violet to see the Vicar to talk to him about her failing marriage. In a scene outside the Vicarage the script had said: 'We watch Richard's car turn into the Vicarage driveway.' We then went inside the Vicarage for a page-and-a-half scene between the Vicar and his wife during which she tells him – having seen the car pull up – that he has a visitor and that it is Hyacinth!

The script then took us back outside again and the directions said: 'Hyacinth and Richard are walking Violet between them. They are talking to Violet and are on their way to the front door of the Vicarage.' The script then called for Violet to stop, distract their attention, break away from them and hurry back to Richard's car. Fine, except that it then said: 'We cut to see the Vicar emerging from the Vicarage. The sight that greets him is Violet with her skirts raised, running quite nimbly for her age. She shoots past the startled Vicar.'

If they had originally left their car and were now on their way to the front door of the Vicarage, how could Violet run back to the car and, on her way, pass the Vicar coming out of the front door for which they had been heading? Please feel free to read this element again but, I promise you, it won't make sense however many times you go over it!

Again, there was far more location material than usual. In fact, I honestly began to wonder whether Roy had got confused between the way *Keeping Up Appearances* was made and *Last of the Summer Wine*. The latter series is totally shot on location (apart from the very few interior scenes that are shot on a film stage), edited and then the finished episode shown to an audience in a cinema – or the radio theatre at Broadcasting House – to pick up their 'reaction'. Whereas *Keeping Up Appearances* was made like a normal sitcom – performed in the studio in front of a live audience who are also shown (in the correct story order) the scenes – normally exteriors – which had been pre-recorded on location.

# EPISODE 6

**Plot:** Hyacinth makes a reluctant Richard take her to a country house auction where she foolishly bids for some wine. This is after Richard has prevented her enthusiastically bidding for other items – which he knows are out of their league and which she wants purely because of their aristocratic associations. They meet up with His Lordship afterwards and the wine proves to be quite strong!

**Cast:** Hyacinth (*Patricia Routledge*); Richard (*Clive Swift*); Liz (*Josephine Tewson*); Daisy (*Judy Cornwell*); Onslow (*Geoffrey Hughes*); Rose (*Mary Millar*); Emmet (*David Griffin*); His Lordship (*Bruce Montague*); Auctioneer (*David Simeon*); Auction Assistant (*David Ashford*); Mrs Braddock (*Jessica James*); His Lordship's Servant (*Colin Stepney*)

**Additional locations:** Some interiors (stairs, corridor, landing, etc.) and ext. stately home (Compton Wyngates, Tysoe). (The auction was in a studio set.)

In this episode there was another full page of dialogue which the script said was heard over the shot of Hyacinth's moving car. There was nothing to be gained from this – only a lot to be lost in terms of Richard's reactions.

In this episode Hyacinth initially mistakes 'His Lordship' for a lesser mortal. Although I didn't do anything about it, this was exactly the same thing that happened with another lord in an episode – also set in a country house – in the first series.

Two pages of this episode – in all three of the copies we were sent – were totally impossible to read due to a printer fault. When my PA contacted Roy's secretary to find out what they should be saying she was clearly given the impression that it hadn't been noticed as these were the only three copies that had been run off – a statement which, sadly, only served to confirm my theory that our writer may never have looked at the finished script.

In this episode there was further proof of my other theory that Roy also seldom watched the series – apart from the recent Christmas Special! As well as not knowing the geography of Hyacinth's bungalow, which I mentioned earlier, there was a scene in this episode where he had Onslow, Daisy and Rose all sitting on their sofa with the dog stretched across them, which would have been extremely difficult because it was very obviously only a small two-seater sofa and always had been since the very first episode five years earlier!

## EPISODE 7

**Plot:** Hyacinth plans to invite Elizabeth and Emmet in for coffee having heard that the latter is directing the local dramatic society's production of *The Boy Friend*, in which she is desperate to have a part. On the other side of town, Daisy is making further attempts to make Onslow feel romantic towards her. However, this has to be put aside, along with Hyacinth's attempts to impress Emmet, when Daddy goes back to his wartime days, stands guard over the house and refuses to let anyone in.

**Cast:** Hyacinth (*Patricia Routledge*); Richard (*Clive Swift*); Liz (*Josephine Tewson*); Daisy (*Judy Cornwell*); Onslow (*Geoffrey Hughes*); Rose (*Mary Millar*); Emmet (*David Griffin*); Vicar (*Jeremy Gittins); Daddy (*George Webb)

**Additional locations:** Coffee shop (The Rocking Horse Coffee Shop, 22 Talisman Sq., Kenilworth)

As Hyacinth needs to impress Emmet with her singing, she rehearses Richard in putting on a certain backing CD for when he and Liz are there later. Because in the past they had always had coffee in the kitchen – and it was unlikely they would have their hi-fi in that room – I thought we might as well make something out of this sudden change. I pointed this out to Roy and he agreed to write the excuse material for having coffee in the lounge. During rehearsals I then added the farcical business – when Daisy rings up interrupting the coffee session – with Hyacinth panicking, bursting into a rendition of 'Sisters' and getting tied up with the phone cable. All of which Pat carried out brilliantly.

Later on when Hyacinth has to drop her plans because Daisy has told her that Daddy is standing guard outside Onslow and Daisy's and won't let them in, there is a group of neighbours watching, to whom Daisy introduces Hyacinth. In the original version the script merely said: 'Daisy introduces Hyacinth to some of her neighbours.' As there was no dialogue provided this would have been extremely dull! When I asked Roy if he could write some dialogue for the introductions he wrote lines for two of the neighbours, which meant that I would have had to employ actors (as distinct from non-speaking 'walk-ons') on full actors' fees for one line each – a bit of a waste of licence payers' money. For this reason I didn't use the amended version but wrote suitable material myself in which Daisy had all the dialogue and briefly explained to Hyacinth who the various people were – getting additional laughs at the same time.

In the original version, in a scene where Onslow is complaining to Richard that Daisy is always trying to get 'romantic', Onslow says to Richard (referring to Hyacinth) 'What would you do if she climbed into your bed?' A rather strange question when the audience knows – even if our writer appeared not to – that from the very start of the series Hyacinth and Richard have always shared a double bed!

There was an amusing moment on location when we were filming Rose, Daisy and Onslow arriving home and taking a secretive look at Daddy on guard outside the house. There is a shot of Rose on her hands and knees peering round the edge of the hedge. When we did this the first time she looked round the hedge and then lost her balance and tumbled forward out of the frame. It only took about five minutes for them to stop laughing sufficiently to enable us to go for a second take!

## EPISODE 8

**Plot:** Hyacinth arrives at the church hall during Emmet's rehearsals of *The Boy Friend* to continue her attempt to get herself a role in the production. Later, she invites Elizabeth and him, plus the Vicar and his wife, to a barbecue she is holding at her sister Violet's home, only to find that once again her sister and brother-in-law are having some terribly loud rows. She hurriedly works out a way of being able to cope with this when her guests arrive – but even the best-laid plans...!

**Cast:** Hyacinth (*Patricia Routledge*); Richard (*Clive Swift*); Liz (*Josephine Tewson*); Daisy (*Judy Cornwell*); Onslow (*Geoffrey Hughes*); Rose (*Mary Millar*); Emmet (*David Griffin*); Vicar (*Jeremy Gittins*); Vicar's Wife (Marion Barron); Man in Phone Box (*Jack Smethurst*); Violet (*Anna Dawson*); Bruce (*John Evitts*); Dancers (*Jenny Morton, Alexander Howard, Anna Bolt*); Daddy (*George Webb*)

**Additional locations:** Int. church hall (Christchurch, Northampton); Violet's home (Newbold Terrace East, Leamington Spa)

143

In this episode the Vicar disappears – having seen Hyacinth's arrival at the church hall during rehearsals – and is eventually discovered by his wife hiding under the stage with three girls from *The Boy Friend* (who are also hiding from Hyacinth). In the original version of the script this scene was set in the same cupboard as the Vicar's wife had found her husband with Rose in an earlier episode. I felt it was bad enough having exactly the same scenario of her finding her husband hiding with females without having it happen in exactly the same place! I changed it to under the stage.

This episode included the first and only time in the entire history of the series that we ever saw Richard really stand up to Hyacinth and shout at her. This happens outside a telephone box when she is unreasonable towards a man who has arrived at the box just before her and needs to make an important call. After Richard tells her off, I wrote the man's comment to Richard: 'In wartime you'd have got a medal for courage like that!' I also wrote Hyacinth's lines as she goes to look for the three girls when she realises that they are no longer listening to her rendition of the title song from the musical *The Boy Friend* plus Elizabeth's line outside the church hall when Hyacinth says she is going inside to surprise Emmet.

During the episode you saw Daddy out with his bucket searching for manure and then passing by Violet's, noticing the cut-outs of horses over the gates and deciding this might be a source of supply. In the original version he suddenly arrives at the barbecue. There was not even the smallest clue as to why he turned up there or what is in the bucket.

I had already warned our writer that Pat wasn't keen on doing too much singing. She certainly had no objection to a snatch here and there but, apart from that, she felt that we had done the joke of her singing badly too often in the past – the main examples being at her own candlelight supper (when Rose turns up unexpectedly) and at the church hall (with Emmet playing the piano for her).

She was also, of course, required to sing badly in the church hall in this episode. However, when this script turned up it also had the whole of the barbecue element hanging on Hyacinth bursting into song every time she thought her guests were liable to overhear Violet and Bruce having a row.

With Roy's blessing I re-wrote it so that, at the appropriate moment, she held up a card with the lyrics written on it and involved her guests in community singing in order to drown out the noise of the argument. I also wrote everything connected with this – setting up the card idea with Richard, writing the lyrics on the cards, explaining it away to her guests as a party game, and, of course, the tag of her suddenly being very concerned because she realises they are singing the same number they have just sung and, in her panic, flinging that card away and it landing on the barbecue and starting the fire. In the original version the barbecue catches fire merely because Richard gets flustered whilst he is cooking.

The original script said (as had been the case several times in the past): 'We can hear that Bruce and Violet are having a row but we can't hear what is being said.' I couldn't help wondering how our writer would have gone about asking the two actors involved to appear to be having a loud slanging match without actually saying anything! He did eventually agree to write some of the specific 'row' speeches which were heard by either Hyacinth or her guests but I had to write the background row dialogue between the specific ones.

There was an unfortunate moment during the filming of the barbecue / community singing scene. At one point Pat got confused over a piece of comedic business and dropped one of the cards. No great problem – I stopped shooting and was perfectly happy to start the shot again. However, I wasn't quite so happy when she commented loudly enough to be heard by a number of the crew and cast – who were all well aware that I had re-written the scene – 'Oh, this is rubbish – it'll never work.' This was not only a very hurtful comment but was also in total contrast to her original reaction on reading my version when she had told me that she had been delighted with the scene. Several of the cast and crew came up to me later and said how much they sympathised with me. Fortunately, her fears were totally unfounded as it did work and got a lot of laughs.


## EPISODE 9

**Plot:** Having entered a local craft fair competition at which she only came second to a lady called Lydia Hawkesworth, Hyacinth is even more put out when she sees the very smart car the lady drives away in. She immediately thinks that she and Richard ought to be moving upmarket car-wise and insists that they call in at a Rolls-Royce showroom. Richard has never driven such an illustrious car before and he certainly has no intention of taking it out for a drive. However, Hyacinth has other ideas!

**Cast:** Hyacinth (*Patricia Routledge*); Richard (*Clive Swift*); Liz (*Josephine Tewson*); Daisy (*Judy Cornwell*); Onslow (*Geoffrey Hughes*); Rose (*Mary Millar*); Emmet (*David Griffin*); Salesman (*Timothy Carlton*); Police Sergeant (*John Pennington*); Daddy (*George Webb*)

**Additional locations:** Craft fair venue (Guy Nelson School Hall, Warwick School); Rolls-Royce showrooms (Lancaster Motors, Northampton); country hotel (Walton Hall, Walton, Wellesbourne)

Even two years earlier when we had been thinking about the fourth series, I had been getting concerned that Hyacinth – in view of her illusions of grandeur – would be extremely unlikely to be happy still being seen driving around in a D-reg car. I had suggested an episode in which she tries to encourage Richard to buy a posh car but, when it becomes obvious they can't afford it, settles for a more realistic new model – or perhaps even a more recent second-hand one – and moves it upmarket with a personalised number plate. This was one of the ideas that I had put forward that Martin Fisher and Pat had liked.

However, as our writer had not used the idea, they still had their old car. As I said earlier, I tactfully reminded him of this again when the fifth series was mooted – on the grounds that I knew that viewers would also be thinking that it was about time they changed their car. When the script for this episode arrived, and I realised it revolved around Hyacinth pushing Richard into looking at new cars, I was delighted because I assumed that this would mean they would finish up with one – but no, they were still left with their old model!

In this episode there was another example of dialogue described as being heard over a long shot of their car – this time *four* whole pages! And not even in attractive countryside.

In the original script Richard expresses no concern that Hyacinth has taken him to a Rolls-Royce garage. He is seen to be totally ignorant of the sort of cars it sells (only Rolls-Royce and Bentleys) despite the fact that it would have logos outside – to say nothing of the obvious presence of very superior vehicles. When I pointed this out to Roy he did agree to change it so that Richard expresses his grave doubts and we see that he is getting worried.

Also in the original version the salesman just casually lets them take the Rolls out for a drive – totally unaccompanied. I thought this was an extremely unlikely scenario and I suspected our viewers would feel the same way. I checked with the sales manager at the Rolls-Royce showroom in Birmingham and, as I suspected, there is absolutely no way – unless they know the customer extremely well because he or she has purchased a previous model from them – that anyone would be allowed to take out a £130,000 Rolls for a run without a member of staff present. He agreed with me that the same would also apply with any, more everyday, car.

I felt that it would surely be funnier and make more sense if the salesman was about to accompany them when he is called away to the phone and five minutes later – when he still hasn't returned – Hyacinth gets impatient and encourages a reluctant Richard not to wait any longer but to drive it anyway. I suggested that we could then have the salesman reporting it to the police as a stolen vehicle. Martin put this to Roy, who, thankfully, agreed with me on this one. I then added in Richard's worries about taking the car; his desire to reverse back into the showroom's area, only for Hyacinth to point out that it was a one-way street; her comment that he couldn't take the next left because it was a 'no entry' and so on – all things that made the initial removal of the car that much more believable. The driver of the car that was behind the Rolls in the one-way street and honking impatiently was my assistant floor manager (i.e. Peter's assistant), Paul Williams.

Incidentally, whenever I had car scenes in an episode – more often than not these involved Richard driving and, of course, Hyacinth telling him how to do so! – I always had a member of my team driving whatever car you see behind Richard's. This is not only for continuity purposes (i.e. to ensure that the car in the background doesn't keep changing), but it also avoids the possibility of an ordinary member of the public following us and the driver or passengers realising we are filming, which can sometimes result in them behaving in an 'exhibitionist' manner.

Anyway, moving on. In this script there were shades of the golfing episode where the Onslow clan turns up at a posh hotel and proceeds to let the side down. In that episode they had at least gone there to pick up Rose, whereas in this one it was a little difficult to believe – with them living on such a meagre budget – that they were likely to turn up at a smart hotel like this. However, it wasn't something of paramount importance. In the original version Hyacinth and Richard hide from Onslow and Daddy at the back of the hotel, having climbed over a hedge between the hotel grounds and some fields. On seeing a tractor approaching they dive into a ditch and are sprayed with manure. They were then supposed to return to the Rolls and drive off.

I suggested that it might be much stronger if they hid from Onslow and Daddy in some other way but still in the hotel grounds before getting back to the Rolls and then, as they are in the process of driving off, they are stopped by a police car (the Rolls having been reported as stolen). When they are outside the Rolls with a policeman taking notes (with Richard being held by another copper), Lydia Hawkesworth – the lady whose posh car Hyacinth has spotted earlier – happens to turn up at the hotel and is met by the sight of Hyacinth in the arms of the law. That would be a strong tag.

In the event I wrote all the 'hiding' material – from the James Bond-style pillar-hiding business right through to them arriving at the car with the fence panel – plus the tag of the episode. As a matter of interest, it was thanks to this episode that Judy fell in love with Jaguars – the car not the animal – because this was the car that Lydia Hawkesworth drives. It was hired for the filming from a Jaguar garage in the area and, when it turned up on location at the hotel, the lady who had delivered it noticed that Judy was showing a great deal of interest. When she was asked if she would like to try the vehicle Judy leapt at the chance and returned saying that it had been an 'orgasmic' experience. She has since purchased one and has remained a Jaguar fan ever since.

## EPISODE 10

**Plot:** In view of the obvious success (in her mind!) of her candlelight suppers, Hyacinth decides to help others by advertising her services as a social hostess in the local paper.

**Cast:** Hyacinth (*Patricia Routledge*); Richard (*Clive Swift*); Liz (*Josephine Tewson*); Daisy (*Judy Cornwell*); Onslow (*Geoffrey Hughes*); Rose (*Mary Millar*); Emmet (*David Griffin*); Milkman (*Robert Rawles*); His Assistant (*John Waterhouse*); Richard's Friend (*Ian Burford*)

**Additional locations:** Ext. no. 24a (129 Market St, Leamington)

Although I had told our writer on several occasions that it would be extremely difficult for us to do any night filming outside Hyacinth's (because of keeping in with the owners and their neighbours), and despite Martin Fisher reminding him of this just three weeks earlier, this script turned up with a scene set outside Hyacinth's at night (in as much as dawn hadn't yet arrived), with dialogue from the milkman actually talking about it being dark. This was subsequently altered.

The major problem in this episode was that of Rose's marriages. We had never referred to her having been married before – in fact in Episode 2 of Series 3 Daisy comments that Rose never gets beyond being a girlfriend and in that same episode Hyacinth says, 'I wish Rose would settle down and find a husband.' However, in this script Daisy and Rose came into the living room with armfuls of Rose's framed wedding photographs, the overall impression being given (assisted by various subsequent dialogue references in several scenes) that Rose could have been married at least half a dozen times!

Apart from the fact that even a light comedy series has to have some basis of reality, I felt that it was extremely unlikely that our viewers, however loyal, could really be expected to suddenly swallow this information. I suggested that it would make much more sense if they were looking back at photos of Rose with men to whom she had been engaged but never actually made it to the altar. Incidentally, to achieve the pictures Daisy and Rose are seen sorting through, we obviously needed to take some shots of the latter with various men, and the first one you see put on the table is of myself with Mary!

There was an amusing moment when Rose and Daisy came into the room carrying the cardboard boxes of photos. As Judy came through the door, her sleeve caught on the handle and she was stopped dead in her tracks. As usual it took quite a time for Onslow and the two girls to stop giggling.

In the original version of Hyacinth telling Richard the content of the telephone call she has just received – following her advertisement in the local paper offering her services as a social hostess – she says: 'My first client, Richard. Twenty men wanting to improve their social graces.' I removed the reference to men because I thought this rather telegraphed the tag of the episode when Hyacinth discovers that her clients were expecting something rather different.

When Hyacinth goes inside to check that she is at the right place for her 'hostessing' there is a scene between Richard and a friend. I wrote this in order to have something happening whilst she was inside. In the original version it didn't exist. Hyacinth went in, Richard gazed into a shop window for a moment or two and then she reappeared. We were supposed to believe that she had gone in, chatted to her 'clients', realised what they thought she was offering and returned to Richard in about ten seconds. I could have made it longer but I doubt whether the audience would really want to spend all that time watching Richard looking into a shop window!

Overall, in this series the episodes had far more location material than ever before. In fact, at one of the studio recordings, we were actually able to make two episodes instead of one because of the amount we had already recorded on location. We finished up with 158 location scenes (some of them lengthy and some quite complicated – on boats etc.) involving 87 *different* locations, which was far in excess of the requirements in the past.

Because of Patricia's involvement with the series *Hetty Wainthropp Investigates*, the start date for the making of this series of *Keeping Up Appearances* had been moved on by six weeks but, in spite of this, the powers-that-be still wanted to begin transmitting the series on the original agreed date, which created quite a few problems. In the past I had always been able to record the episodes (studio-wise) in the order that was the most economical. This was particularly the case when an episode involved additional artistes who would be needed both on location and in the studio, which meant that they had to be paid a retainer fee for the period between the two elements – unless they happened to have other work (which, quite often, wasn't the case).

In the past, to reduce this period – and the relevant payment – as much as possible, I had always planned things so that the studio recordings of these episodes were the first ones that we did when we returned from the location filming. This meant that there was as small a gap as possible between the two elements, which saved the BBC a lot of money in retainer fees. Also, in the past, by having quite a few of the episodes fully completed by the date when the series started to transmit, I was able to arrange for them to go out in an order that reduced the chances of the public realising that elements of some of the storylines were, shall we say, rather similar ... well, all right, repetitive! I was now being forced into a corner where I was only ever going to be one episode ahead of transmission, which made life extremely difficult.

Rather late in the day the powers-that-be suddenly asked for a Christmas episode for 1995. In view of Pat's very limited availability because of the drama series and her not unreasonable desire to have a couple of weeks' break between the end of that and starting with us, I just knew I wouldn't be able to fit in any more location material and, after nine weeks in the studio, there would be no way we could all traipse back to Leamington and Coventry and brave the inclement weather. Besides which, Pat would certainly be pretty exhausted by that time. I therefore had no alternative but to tell Roy that, regrettably, the Christmas episode couldn't contain any location work or, at least, the absolute minimum. Because I suspected that coming up with an episode with this proviso might flummox our writer, I suggested to Martin Fisher that the following storyline might be a possible idea.

## Christmas Episode 1995

It is the morning of Christmas Eve and, having returned from the shops with the turkey, etc., Hyacinth invites the usual reluctant

Liz and Emmet in for coffee and, whilst they are with her, learns that they won't be able to come to her Boxing Day drinks 'do' after all because they are now going to relatives for Christmas. Once they've left, Hyacinth starts checking through her elaborate plans for the next few days. Looking at her guest list for drinks on Boxing Day morning her conscience starts to prick her and she wonders whether her seasonal spirit should extend as far as including Onslow, Daisy, Rose and Daddy. She very quickly decides that it shouldn't!

The weather is freezing that night and she and Richard are in bed in the small hours of Christmas morning when they are awoken by the sound of running water. As they go into the hall, they see water seeping under the kitchen door and, on going into the kitchen, they discover to their horror that a pipe has burst and they are awash with three inches of water. We see them slopping about in their bare feet and Hyacinth trying to organise Richard – who has sensibly turned off the electrics and is now looking under the sink, using a torch and trying to turn off the mains stopcock, which doesn't seem to want to move.

We see them delve into the *Yellow Pages* and try to ring plumbers but they are all out answering other emergency calls. We could see Hyacinth on the telephone remonstrating with the plumber's other halves as to why her emergency is much more important than all the others! Richard eventually manages to turn the stopcock off – with great difficulty because of the hard water deposits which Hyacinth says she is going to take up with her MP and, if necessary, the Prime Minister – but, as daylight dawns, it is very obvious that Hyacinth's Christmas plans have been well and truly put out.

What are they going to do – where are they going to go? Elizabeth and Emmet have gone away and suddenly Hyacinth realises that they don't have any other friends! Daisy rings up on Christmas morning to wish them the compliments of the season and Richard answers the phone and tells her the events of the night. Daisy insists that they come and spend Christmas with them and, in the circumstances, it is obviously impossible to find a suitable excuse.

We would then see Hyacinth reluctantly tucking into Daisy's idea of Christmas lunch, drinking Onslow's idea of good wine, and in the afternoon, being coerced into playing rowdy party games, perhaps with a few of Daisy and Onslow's friends – with Rose, in the background, giggling and behaving romantically under the mistletoe with two different men. Thank heavens Christmas only comes but once a year!

Note: Once I have finished the studio recordings of the ten episodes comprising series five, I would be able to find time to pre-record the flooded kitchen scene on a 'film' stage in the London area and then have the normal rehearsal period and studio recording for the other scenes involved – all of which are interiors.

Martin Fisher seemed to like the proposed storyline but our writer was not keen. Instead, he came up with the following:

## CHRISTMAS SPECIAL 1995

**Plot:** Hyacinth takes over the running of the church's annual pageant only to find that all the people who had originally volunteered to be involved disappear!

**Cast:** Hyacinth (*Patricia Routledge*); Richard (*Clive Swift*); Liz (*Josephine Tewson*); Daisy (*Judy Cornwell*); Onslow (*Geoffrey Hughes*); Rose (*Mary Millar*); Emmet (*David Griffin*); Vicar (*Jeremy Gittins*); Vicar's Wife (*Marion Barron*); Mrs Moody (*Una Stubbs*); Violet (*Anna Dawson*); Bruce (*John Evitts*); Shop Assistant (*Miranda Kingsley*); Mr Crabtree (*Tony Stuart*); Daddy (*George Webb*)

As agreed there was a minimum amount of location material – Hyacinth being put into the back of the ambulance outside the church hall – and, owing to the lack of studio space, Onslow in the wine merchant's. I did write a bit of extra material – particularly in the scene where Elizabeth and Richard are ironing costumes and I added all the ancestral details Emmet gives Hyacinth and Richard about the

French queen of England. However, in the light of my experience with the Christmas show the previous year, I kept my contribution to a minimum.

When Patricia first read the script she was understandably rather concerned about the element where Elizabeth – who is working backstage – undoes the wrong rope and a background cloth falls on top of Hyacinth. However, I took a great deal of trouble to get my designer to arrange things so that the usual timber baton at the base of the cloth was actually rubber and 'no actors were hurt during the making of this episode'. There were a few comments made afterwards by certain people connected with the programme agreeing that I was certainly right to change the timber base but asking – in view of her remark about my script in the barbecue sequence in Episode 8 – why I hadn't changed it to lead! I assume they were joking.

There was an amusing moment in a scene between Hyacinth and Emmet. Once he has addressed her as 'Your Majesty' she goes into a lot of silly French patter, shaking her head as she does so. We had to do a retake of this because the first time round she jiggled her head about so much that her crown fell off.

It was not the most successful episode and, as I said earlier, statistics proved that it wasn't anything like as popular with the viewers as the previous years 'special' of which I had written such a large amount.

Overall, the filming period for the fifth series went very smoothly. At one point we had to leave Leamington to travel to Great Yarmouth where we were going to film the seaside element – funfair etc. – of the pensioners' day out episode.

We were there for four days – including shooting the various elements of their journey down to the coast in the mini-bus – and on one of these, whilst we were filming at the funfair, I saw Pat intently watching members of the public enjoying themselves on the roller-coaster and the log ride, both of which were obviously very popular. Noting her interest, I mentioned that myself, Peter and my cameraman had been on the rides in question the night before and that it had been great fun. On hearing this Pat looked quite envious and I asked if she would also like to have a go. Her response was very much in the affirmative and I suggested that the two of us could do so after the end of filming the following day if she still fancied the idea. This suggestion obviously appealed to her enormously.

The next day, after we'd got back to the hotel and watched the rushes, I suggested that we met up again at 8.15 and then return to the funfair and enjoy ourselves. She agreed very enthusiastically. At 7.55 the telephone rang in my bedroom and it was Pat enquiring what she should wear. I said that it didn't really matter – especially as we were going to get wet – to which she commented that she had to think of her public. In the event, when I met her in reception, she was wearing a sort of pink tracksuit. As the funfair was only about three hundred yards along the promenade I had assumed that we would walk but she said she would rather we used my car – presumably so 'her public' wouldn't see her strolling along in a tracksuit.

In the meantime I had told Peter that Pat and I were going on the two rides at the funfair and he went ahead of us with my camera to catch her un-Hyacinth-like activities. Pat, Peter and myself went on the roller-coaster with all of us hanging on for dear life and screaming as one does. Pat and I then approached the water ride. I went on slightly ahead and had a quick confidential word with the attendant and asked him where one needed to sit in order to get the wettest. He obviously realised what I had in mind and told me that, surprisingly, you got a lot wetter in the rear of the 'log'.

I casually suggested to Pat that, as there were only two of us, she should sit in the back and myself in the front. She said that she was quite happy for me to sit in the front but she'd sit immediately behind me. Whilst we both got pretty wet, my presence, immediately in front of her as she clung on to me, at least protected her to a degree.

When we came off the ride Pat was really happy and used a towel she had brought with her from the hotel to dry my hair or at least what's left of it! (I'm sure I had a lot more before I started on *Keeping Up Appearances*.) When we got back into my car Patricia threw her arms around me, gave me a kiss and said that she hadn't enjoyed herself so much for years.

The location work was going very well and Patricia was obviously much happier with my version of the scripts. In fact, it had been reported to me from three different sources that she had been heard to comment during the filming that, thanks to all the work I had done on the scripts, they had finished up so much better and, as a result, she might well consider doing a further batch 'out of loyalty to her public'.

Because I had been told this, I casually asked her, as I was driving her back to the unit hotel about four weeks into the filming, whether she would consider making a sixth series. Her response was that she wouldn't be able to fit it in the following year because she was appearing at the theatre in Chichester but it might be a possible the year after that and she would think about it.

Incidentally, whilst we were away on location we heard that David Liddiment – the Head of Entertainment – was leaving the BBC to become Head of ITV Network Control. The last time we had spoken (or rather *he* had spoken!) was when he had torn into me for altering the 1994 Christmas Special. As I wouldn't be seeing him before he left, I dropped him a line telling him that, since that stormy meeting, Roy had not only used a storyline of mine but had also told me to make any alterations to the ten scripts that I thought were necessary! David responded a few days later with a three-line note wishing me luck with the series but making absolutely no comment about our writer's change of attitude and my having to do exactly what I had done in the past!

We got back to London and started rehearsals as usual. Everything went very well – as did the recordings. I was used to being extremely busy in my role of producer/director but this was especially the case with this batch of programmes because each episode was being transmitted just one week after we had been in the studio. This meant that I had the added pressure of having it edited, dubbed and so on within a few days, whilst, of course, at the same time, rehearsing the next one.

When I was giving Patricia a lift back to Television Centre after one of the rehearsal days for the burglar alarm episode – the idea of mine which Pat particularly liked and thought worked very well – I again tentatively raised the subject of the possibility of a sixth series. Had she had any further thoughts since we last discussed it?

It didn't seem that unreasonable to ask her because it had been several weeks since I had first mentioned it and, in the meantime, it was obvious from the viewing figures that this batch of programmes was being very well received by the viewing public. Also, of course, the BBC was keen to know and, until Patricia had made a decision, her fellow actors couldn't be sure where they stood and felt, not unreasonably, that they probably wouldn't be considered for other long-term projects until the future of *Keeping Up Appearances* was known. I wasn't asking Patricia to arrive at specific dates; I was merely enquiring whether she had come to a decision since our earlier chat.

I am perfectly happy to admit that I also had a vested interest. She, however, still didn't have an answer.

A week or so later I was told that *Keeping Up Appearances* had won the Netherlands' coveted Silver Tulip Award for Best Foreign Programme. There was going to be an awards ceremony at their studios in Amsterdam and they wanted Patricia to attend and accept the award. In the event this wasn't very practical because, on the date in question, we were going to be in the middle of rehearsing a particularly busy episode which had less than usual pre-recorded location material. Pat, therefore, had a lot more to learn and, quite reasonably, didn't feel that she could spare the time to fly to Holland and attend the ceremony. As I was the show's producer/director, they then asked me to go instead and I did so – leaving at the end of one of the rehearsal days and flying straight out to the venue.

It was a wonderful glamorous evening with an excellent dinner and a huge floorshow. I was made very welcome and the award was presented to me by a multi-millionaire businessman who 'flew' down onto the stage from inside the roof of the vast studio sitting on a huge rocket! After staying the night I flew back the following morning (in a conventional plane – not a rocket!), was met at Heathrow by a hire car and was whizzed to rehearsals where I showed the cast the award.

We completed the ten episodes but didn't have the end-of-series party then because we were due back in the studios a couple of weeks later to make the Christmas Special and I decided that it would be more appropriate to hold it then.

However, as we had reached the end of the run of the ten episodes, when I went to see Pat in her dressing room after the recording (as I always did) I thought it might be a reasonable time to enquire whether she had now come to a decision about another series. She said she hadn't. I discovered a few months later that at the times I had asked Pat about the possibility of a further series, the BBC still hadn't made its mind up as to whether it wanted to proceed with a second series of *Hetty Wainthropp Investigates*. By not categorically saying that she wouldn't consider playing Hyacinth any more, perhaps Pat was rather cleverly hedging her bets. It was, after all, a rather strange coincidence that, as soon as she was offered a contract for a second series of *Hetty*, she declared that 'Hyacinth' was over and thus brought a very successful project to an end. Ironically, quite a few years later, in 2008, there was an article in the *Daily Mail* in which Patricia Routledge criticised the BBC over the way the cast of *Hetty Wainthropp Investigates* were not kept informed as to whether there was going to be a fifth series – which there wasn't. 'How rude!' she says in the article. Perhaps she now knows how I and the cast of *Keeping Up Appearances* felt when she kept us in the dark!

Rehearsals continued for the Christmas Special and after the recording we had the end-of-series party. It was particularly moving and sad because we were all ninety-nine per cent sure that this was our last time together. At the party I made my usual speech thanking the crew, the make-up, costume and design staff, the three members of my production team who, as usual had been wonderful, and, of course, the very talented cast.

When I had finished I sat down, there was a thirty-seconds pause and then Clive stood up, asked for a bit of hush and then, rather falteringly, said some very nice things about me and also commented on the huge contribution that I had made to the series. Everyone applauded and we moved on to looking at the 'out-takes', which, as usual, created a lot of laughs.

When we began to say our goodbyes it was quite emotional – especially between myself and members of the cast because we had spent so much time together during the previous six years. There were lots of warm hugs and kisses between us, although, sadly, Patricia didn't seem to be all that moved by the occasion.

The following day I rang Clive at home and thanked him for the nice things he had said about me. He apologised for having been rather hesitant and said that, had he known in advance that he was going to make a speech, he would have prepared something and, therefore, been rather more fluent. He went on to tell me that, after I had made my speech, he had turned to Pat and whispered, 'Aren't you going to say something about Harold?', to which she had said 'No'. He told me that he had been so embarrassed and just couldn't believe that she didn't want to say anything about the person who had given her the part of Hyacinth – and who had also done so much, way beyond the normal duties of a producer/director, to make the show the success that it had become.

However, I still have on my study wall (alongside framed photos – with messages – of a host of other artistes with whom I worked over the years), a framed picture of Patricia as Hyacinth which she had given me after the first series. On it she had written 'To Harold, with gratitude and enormous admiration – and love from Patricia Routledge' and then in brackets: 'Her first sitcom and they *told* me you'd be wonderful!'

Anyway, that was that – *Keeping Up Appearances* was over. Incidentally – apart from *Last of the Summer Wine*, it was the longest-running series that Roy Clarke wrote.

Although Roy had been responsible for a number of different shows over the years (including *Open All Hours*), it is quite interesting that six of them never made it beyond the first series.

Despite all the problems, *Keeping Up Appearances* was a great success and continues to be extremely popular both in the UK and in many other countries around the world. Roy came up with some wonderful characters. Patricia played the part of Hyacinth brilliantly and was supported by a wonderful cast and I loved working with them all.

I hope you have found it interesting going 'behind the scenes'.

# Moving On

In the summer of 1995 Martin Fisher had ceased to be Head of Comedy and had been replaced by Geoffrey Perkins, whose idea of popular situation comedy was somewhat different from people like myself. He seemed to prefer rather more 'off the wall' material which, on the whole, appealed to the younger generation but left the mainstream audience for situation comedy – generally people aged about forty upwards – feeling deprived and thoroughly fed up with what they were being offered. It would be fair to say that it was not all his fault – suddenly everyone seemed to think that, because a series called *Men Behaving Badly* had been a success (and, of its type, it was very good), everything from then on had to be 'outrageous', involve a young cast and have fairly large helpings of bad behaviour, swearing, lager louts and vomit jokes.

I'm not saying that television shouldn't cater for younger viewers, but suddenly everything went in that direction and virtually nothing was available for the main fans of situation comedy. The type of show that had characters with whom the main audience for the genre could associate –– which is a large part of its success – was deemed to be old-fashioned and 'obsolete'. Those characters were seen as 'stereotypes'. It almost seemed to have become more important for something to be 'different' than funny. Because the 'new' things didn't go down particularly well, the audience figures, understandably, dropped.

Repeats of *Keeping Up Appearances* and other shows of similar standing gained higher viewing figures than the new programmes on offer. Instead of the powers-that-be realising – or admitting – that this was because a large part of the audience didn't like what they were now being offered, they came out with the statement that situation comedy was obviously dead and no longer required! It never seemed to occur to them that it wasn't dead – it was just that they were killing it off!

Anyway, moving on. In the last couple of months of my time at the BBC I was shown a script that Roy had apparently sent in a few months earlier. It was a spin-off of *Keeping Up Appearances* revolving around the Onslow crowd having new neighbours who were upset by what was going on in the world of Daisy, Onslow and Rose. I was asked to read it but I found it very disappointing. It seemed that Roy was doing exactly the same sort of thing that he had done with Hyacinth but, this time, it was far less believable because it was all happening on a council estate.

Whilst I totally agreed that there might well still be an interest in Onslow et al. – fan letters proved this – I felt that much more could be gained from it than by just having a low-class Hyacinth move in next door. I was also concerned that there would no longer be any reason for seeing the characters of Elizabeth and Emmet, who were also extremely popular with the viewers.

I came up with the version you will find in Appendix 2. The BBC liked this very much but Roy, unfortunately, didn't. He commented that the idea of Onslow out of context didn't work for him.

Three months later – and after almost forty years with the BBC, the last twenty-eight producing and directing some extremely successful comedies for them – I had to 'retire'.

The BBC held a wonderful leaving party for me and, at a special dinner afterwards, I was presented with an album which Susan, my excellent PA, had organised. Apparently this had never been done before for anyone else but it was thought to be very appropriate in my case. Unbeknown to me Susan had talked to my wife, Jean, and had asked her for the names of various people – artiste-wise – whose series I had directed over the years and she had then contacted the people in question.

It was a lovely idea and, as a result, the album contained letters and photos with wonderful messages from a number of people including Ronnie Barker, Richard Wilson, Nigel Havers, Leslie Phillips, Richard Briers, Tony Britton, Peter Egan, Dinah Sheridan, June Whitfield, Francis Matthews, Ray Cooney, Susan Hampshire, Penelope Wilton, among others. I was sorry that Susan hadn't been able to contact the likes of Dick Emery, Roy Castle, Roy Kinnear and Marti Caine, but she came up with some feeble excuse! (For those of you who are not aware of the real reason, they had, sadly, passed on.)

It also included, of course, lovely messages from the cast of *Keeping Up Appearances* – that is everyone except Patricia! Susan subsequently contacted her again, tactfully saying that perhaps her original letter asking Patricia to contribute had gone astray but she still never heard anything. Because the album was no longer a 'surprise', I then rang up Pat myself and asked if she would contribute and she said she might do so but I heard nothing. A few months later I wrote to her reminding her of our conversation but, to this day, she still hasn't contributed to the album.

In 1996, a year after I had retired from the BBC, I was asked by the American side of BBC Worldwide to put together a compilation based around a diary that Hyacinth had supposedly kept. The end result was going to be called *The Memoirs of Hyacinth Bucket* and shown on America's PBS channel during their pledge weeks to raise funds from the viewers.

I accepted this task and sat down with my VHS tapes of all the episodes, selected umpteen possible extracts, narrowed them down, listed some of Hyacinth's best-known characteristics and decided which extracts best depicted those traits. I then wrote all the material that Hyacinth was supposed to have been written in her diary.

It was planned that the various extracts would be linked by Daisy and Onslow and I suggested that the former could have gained access to the diary because Hyacinth had accidentally included it amongst some old photo albums she had lent Daisy. I then asked Roy to write this linking material. He agreed to do so and a contract was drawn up. However, when his script arrived I had some reservations about it which I put to him. He faxed me the following day saying that there was nothing wrong with his script.

I sent the script to America but the executives of BBC Worldwide in New York contacted me because they also had reservations about certain elements so I, therefore, re-wrote various sections. These were accepted enthusiastically, enabling the project to go ahead.

I did the necessary filming with Geoffrey and Judy, edited the whole thing together with Andy – titles, links, extracts, and so on – and sent it off to the States. BBC Worldwide was extremely happy with the end result, as was PBS. A few weeks later I was telephoned by the BBC's American office to say that the programme had been so well received that they were now planning to sell it to certain other countries. They also wanted to turn it into a video. I recontracted everyone involved to cover this additional outlet and the video is still selling very well.

Knowing, as I did, that Her Majesty, the Queen Mother, was a great fan of the series, I sent her a copy for her hundredth birthday in August 2000. Her private secretary wrote back saying that Her Majesty had taken the tape to Scotland with her and she was very much looking forward to watching it.

A few years after her death, informal photographs of the Queen Mother taken in her Scottish home by a member of her staff, clearly showed videos of *Keeping Up Appearances* on a nearby table.

In 1998 I was told by Geoffrey Perkins that he had had lunch with Patricia a few days earlier and that he had gained the distinct impression that she might not be averse to doing a 'one-off' special – providing the storyline was strong and sufficiently different from the episodes we had made in the past. In case Roy wouldn't be able to come with something strong enough to interest Patricia, I spent several days working out an outline, which Geoffrey liked – although he had a couple of minor reservations. (You can find this in Appendix 3.) I then sent a copy to Patricia with a little note saying that I had gathered from Geoffrey that she might not be against doing a 'one-off' special and asking what she thought of the idea I was enclosing.

Three months later I still hadn't heard from her. When I finally asked her agent if she could get her client to ring me, Patricia eventually did so telling me in no uncertain terms that Geoffrey Perkins had obviously got the wrong impression – there was absolutely no way she wanted to play Hyacinth again.

As with my other series over the years I have remained good friends with the other members of the cast of *Keeping Up Appearances*. We keep in touch, often chat and sometimes meet up for a meal together. It so happens that Judy's husband, John, shares the same birthday as me. So, for some years now, we alternate the celebrations by my wife and me going to them one year and them coming to us the next year.

Incidentally, as well as being a very competent actress, Judy Cornwell is also an established author. In fact, during the time she was with us making *Keeping Up Appearances* she wrote – and had published – two of her novels, *The Seventh Sunrise* and *Fear and Favours*.

In 1998 we learned the very sad news of the death of Mary Millar (Rose). During the weeks leading up to this – when she wasn't at all well – I spoke to her regularly on the telephone and I was honoured to be asked by her husband and daughter to read Mary's favourite psalm at her memorial service at All Souls Church, London. David Griffin unfortunately wasn't able to attend because he was working up North but all the rest of the cast were present – except Patricia. She seems to have lost touch with the members of the cast and myself, in spite of all of us having worked together extremely closely for six years – which, in show business, is a very long time.

To move on for the last time. Way back in 1996, Geoffrey Perkins had told me that he thought there was a very strong chance that the BBC would want to make a special episode of *Keeping Up Appearances* to mark the millennium. He was also pretty sure that Patricia would agree in view of the fact that it would commemorate such an important event. In the early part of 1999 I sat down and came up with a possible storyline for this (Appendix 4).

Geoffrey told me he thought it was very good and that he would put the idea to Roy Clarke and, if he liked it, Geoffrey would then contact Patricia's agent. I never heard another thing about this.

When, out of interest, I rang Roy Clarke in December 1999, he told me that no one had mentioned anything to him about the possibility of a Millennium Special. I then rang Patricia's agent who told me that the subject had been mooted but Patricia didn't want to have anything more to do with the series. It seems so sad that she didn't wish to get together again with the other members of the cast and myself to provide the many millions of loyal fans of the series with just one 'special' episode to mark a 'one-off' occasion.

A few years after the final series of *Keeping Up Appearances*, BBC Scotland came up with a series called *Comedy Connections*. Each episode looked at a different comedy series from the past, and together with a few clips there were interviews with members of the cast, writers and directors who had been involved. It also informed the public which shows the various participants had done both before and after the series they were featuring that week. I was asked to take part on the programmes they made covering *Dad's Army, Don't Wait Up, Ever Decreasing Circles* and, of course, *Keeping Up Appearances.*

Although myself, Roy Clarke and all the ether members of the cast took part, Patricia declined to do so and, instead, they had to resort to using bits of various interviews that she had done in the past! A bit sad and it was obviously rather strange having a specific series being covered without the star participating.

# *Appendices*

## APPENDIX 1: SUGGESTED STORYLINES FOR SERIES 4

These are the storylines I was asked to send to Roy Clarke for the fourth series, along with the one involving the *QE2* that was used:

### i What about personalised number plates?

At breakfast one morning Hyacinth comes into the kitchen with the post and tells Richard that Mr Philpot down the road has obviously sold his car and brought another – a BMW. She comments that their own car is a D reg and surely the time has come to change it. Richard says that they can't afford to and, anyway, it runs perfectly well.

By chance, as part of their mail, there is a letter from what is obviously a timeshare company – more or less offering them a fifty–fifty chance of being given a new Volvo if they attend a meeting. Throwing all caution to the wind, Hyacinth tells Richard that they ought to attend as it definitely looks as if there is a fair chance of finishing up with a new car. Richard tries to explain that the whole business is suspect but, with her eyes on a new car for 'nothing', Hyacinth is determined. She rings up, tells them which session they will attend and they do so – albeit with Richard far from keen and sensing trouble.

On these occasions the 'sharks' do everything they can to wear down their potential customers. This involves hanging on to people for a couple of hours at least whilst they are bombarded with information. However, in Hyacinth's case – because of the very awkward questions she is asking about their 'wonderful offer', and what the 'catch' is – and, concerned that she is likely to encourage other people at the meeting to do the same thing, they can't wait to get rid of her. When she refuses to be fobbed off with the 'crystal' decanter she is given for attending (the lowest item and the one they normally give people), she is offered a portable TV – anything (apart from the obviously 'fictitious' car) just as long as she goes!

Later, as Richard is turning the pages of his newspaper, Hyacinth suddenly spots a whole-page advert for personalised number plates, which gives her an idea. A special number plate would make all the difference to their present car – after all, who does Richard know round here who has a personal number plate?

She pops next door and asks Liz, but neither she nor Emmet know anybody with special plates. Now totally hooked on the idea, Hyacinth discusses with Richard what initials they should aim for. At first she naturally fancies 'HB', but reluctantly settles for 'RB' when Richard points out that, although she does the back-seat driving, he is the one actually at the wheel. She looks at the advert in detail – with the aid of a magnifying glass because the print is so small (as it generally is) – and can't find any reference to 'RB'.

She telephones the firm and they are adamant they don't have 'RB1' available. She reports back to Richard, who says that he never thought that 'RB1' would be available. He casually comments that some people have their initials but go for a higher number because they intend it to match the number of cars they have owned. Hyacinth immediately likes this idea because, if there was a higher number available, they could, at the same time, give the impression that this is their tenth, twelfth or perhaps even fifteenth car!

With renewed enthusiasm she rings the firm back and systematically enquires about the same initials but sequential numbers and, from her end of the conversation, it sounds like an auction. She is told that that there are no 'RB' numbers available and won't be until the present holders decide to give theirs up for some reason.

With a sudden thought that she has seen some combination of 'HRB' somewhere recently, Hyacinth rings Daisy to enquire what the number plate is on the old banger in their front garden – Onslow can't remember and is far too engrossed in the telly to look out of the window so Daisy obliges. The number has no connection with 'HRB' and Hyacinth refuses to tell Daisy why she is interested. We could stay at Daisy's after Hyacinth rings off as they wonder whether

Hyacinth has taken up number-plate spotting as a hobby – will it be trains next?

Later, we find Hyacinth scanning a copy of *Debrett's Distinguished People of Today* (which she has borrowed) and from which she is coming up with a list of names of people who might have RB number plates.

She reads the list to Richard: Richard Baker, Roger Bannister ('Why does he need a car – he runs everywhere, doesn't he?'), Rodney Bewes, Richard Biffa ('He's into 'Disposal' – perhaps he wants to get rid of his number plate') and Richard Briers. She asks Richard – who is getting really annoyed by now – if he can think of any more whilst she puts the kettle on and he facetiously comes with Ronnie Biggs, the Red Barron and Russell & Bromley!

Hyacinth sets about trying to track some of these people down. She rings Richard Briers' agent (whose number is in the Debrett book) but a secretary understandably doesn't know whether he has a special number plate or not. Unfortunately, when Hyacinth asks how long it will be before he could be asked, the girl casually lets it drop that Richard Briers is recording at the BBC that day. Hyacinth rings the BBC, gives the distinct impression that it is extremely urgent, and we see Richard Briers (dressed in some Shakespearean costume) take the call on a studio 'wall phone' (or perhaps he is in the process of changing in his dressing room) and his subsequent reaction to being telephoned on a hectic recording day by this insane woman. (As I worked with Richard for two years I know him very well and there was every chance that he would play ball – subject to his availability.)

Hyacinth rings the firm again and, now somewhat desperate, asks them to check what they have available with any RB connotation and ring her back. As it happens, when they do so, Richard answers the call and, with some amusement, he tells Hyacinth that all they have to offer is 'ROB 7 NIT' and 'RUB 2 TIT'. She reluctantly accepts that she had better forget the whole thing and settles for having the car professionally waxed and polished instead and – brilliant idea – some new headed notepaper.

We leave her looking at the Debrett book again to try and decide on someone important to write to in order to copy their notepaper when they respond – as, of course, they are bound to on receiving a letter from her!

(Obviously if it is felt that the inclusion of the timeshare element is going to make this episode overlong, then it can be dropped.)

## ii The family tree

Hyacinth intercepts the morning mail, explaining to the postman that she is waiting for a reply from a firm that she has written to that traces one's family tree and any possible coat of arms. As it happens, the postman does have the firm's response and Hyacinth can't wait to open it. She sits Richard down but her face drops as she reads the contents. The news is not good – there seems to be very little trace of anything remotely worth boasting about. Richard suggests that perhaps he should have his ancestry traced instead but this idea is rapidly dismissed.

There is a telephone call from Daisy and we discover that when Hyacinth happened to let it drop a fortnight ago that she had written to this company, Daisy and Rose had clubbed together and done the same thing as a birthday present for Onslow. Their reply has also arrived that morning and it transpires that Onslow's ancestors came over with the Normans and that there have been several aristocratic connections over the years. His family also have a long-lost coat of arms.

Hyacinth is furious and is convinced that the firm has obviously made a simple error about herself but is definitely wrong about Onslow! She decides to delve into her background herself. She discovers Daisy has a copy of their family tree, which Onslow reluctantly goes into the loft to bring down and then takes it over to Hyacinth. She studies this very carefully (alongside the details sent her by the 'Ancestral' company) and sees that there is no note of her great-grandmother ever having married – although she did have a child. She subsequently makes a telephone call to some obscure aunt, who passes her on to an even more obscure elderly cousin from whom Hyacinth discovers, to her horror, that her great-grandmother was a chambermaid at a downmarket inn and had a brief affair with the pot man.

Hyacinth is determined to change this story – as we hear when

Elizabeth is invited in for tea that afternoon. Whilst admitting to her great-grandmother being the housekeeper at a large fashionable hotel – 'far too young to be doing such a responsible job' – she changes the story to the fact that her great-grandmother was unbelievably pretty – in fact, 'totally irresistible', apparently – and was quite understandably taken advantage of by a duke who was staying at the hotel.

### iii The new council tax

Richard is busy writing cheques, and moaning about paying bills – the telephone account (Sheridan reversing the charges, Hyacinth ringing lots of people, generally to complain about something), Barclaycard ('What was this amount for?') and various regular monthly payments –gas, electricity (if she feels cold during the day, why can't she wear a cardigan instead of putting the heating on to 'constant'? Hyacinth says she couldn't do that – supposing someone called! He takes her to the meter cupboard and shows her the little wheel whizzing around) and, of course, his monthly payment covering the new Council Tax. He comments that Elizabeth's property is presumably in the same 'band' and wonders whether Emmet pulls his weight with his share of the burden.

We see that Hyacinth has been deeply shocked at the thought of their property being on the same band as Elizabeth's and she asks the latter in for coffee and casually brings up the subject. It turns out to be true (which worries Hyacinth enormously), but Elizabeth then innocently mentions that she's heard that poor Mr Ellis down the road has an even greater problem because apparently his property has been placed in a higher band than theirs.

This doesn't go down well with Hyacinth. After all the trouble she has taken over the years to be 'one up', this man has the audacity to have a property in a higher 'band' than hers! Without telling Richard, she goes to the council and sees an official who assumes, understandably, that she is going to be yet another person complaining that they are on the wrong band. She admits this is the case but then amazes the official by asking for their property to go up a band. In fact, in an ideal world, two bands! She wants it done as soon as possible and the stunned official says he will deal with it immediately.

This could then develop into a situation with Richard receiving a new assessment in the next day's post – Hyacinth is out at the time – and the various ramifications as he checks with a few neighbours (including Emmet) to find out if *they've* been reassessed before ringing up to complain to the council. He tells Emmet that he's not going to let Hyacinth know that he's complained because he only told her off the day before for using the telephone for that purpose.

Because of the general confusion – Richard has said there is no way that he asked for it to be raised – an official makes an appointment to come round that afternoon and look at the property for himself. Hyacinth returns just as the man arrives and before Richard has a chance to tell her why the man is here the telephone rings and, whilst Richard answers it, the official merely tells Hyacinth that he has come round to check that they are in the correct band.

She leaps at the opportunity of showing the property off and starts to give him a tour round, pointing out and, of course, elaborating on all the 'plus' features of the property. As Richard puts the telephone down (it was a call in connection with something he has ordered by mail order) and starts to return the phone rings again and he has to answer it once more. It is Sheridan.

Meanwhile, Hyacinth is still doing her tour of the property, going out of her way to impress the official. The front door bell rings and she goes white when she discovers it is Onslow, Daisy and Rose who have turned up at quite the wrong moment and are obviously going to let the tone of the place down. She hurriedly bundles them into a room that she has already shown the official. Richard comes off the phone and realises, to his horror, that Hyacinth is 'selling' the place to the official. He then sees Onslow's car outside, suspects they must be indoors somewhere, gets them out of the room and proceeds to use them to create exactly the opposite picture to the one being painted by Hyacinth!

### iv Win a candlelit supper
A notice appears in local paper saying that they are trying to raise funds for a special cause and inviting suggestions for so doing. Hyacinth telephones the editor and suggests that they run a competition – for which people pay a small entry fee – with the first prize being an

invitation to attend a very special candlelight supper prepared by the local expert in such things – Hyacinth Bouquet. She would set the questions – most of which could be based on etiquette and social niceties. The newspaper promises to send someone round to interview her. She has visions of someone important – the paper's own Nigel Dempster – but it turns out to be a cub reporter on his first job.

Hyacinth involves Richard in deciding the questions that should be posed and then calls round to Daisy and Onslow in order to check that they (and those of a similar 'status') would definitely be unable to answer them. After all, she tells Richard, we don't want someone 'unsuitable' winning and coming to my 'superior' candlelight supper.

She is subsequently extremely put out to discover that no one has decided to enter that particular competition, although several rival fund-raising ideas are apparently faring extremely well. She tries phoning people up to encourage them to enter but there are no takers – Elizabeth gets out of it by saying that she isn't bright enough to answer the brilliant questions that Hyacinth has so cleverly posed. Emmet goes into hiding – although Hyacinth has gone to great pains to ensure that some of the questions are of a musical nature.

Eventually, in order to avoid the newspaper publishing the fact that no one has shown any interest, Hyacinth enters under an assumed name and wins her own supper.

## v Hyacinth has Emmet to stay

We start with Liz being ushered in for coffee on some pretext and hear Hyacinth enquiring how the work Elizabeth is having done next door is progressing. We learn that Liz is decorating and also having built-in furniture installed in her bedroom. During the upheaval she has moved into Emmet's room and he has been sleeping in the lounge for a few days.

Elizabeth tells Hyacinth that unfortunately that morning, during the alterations, some very suspect wiring has been discovered and a lot of the lounge floorboards will have to be taken up for a couple of days, which will make it impossible for Emmet to continue to sleep in the lounge as planned.

Much to Liz's horror (how she wishes she hadn't said anything!),

Hyacinth immediately invites Emmet to stay with Richard and her for a couple of nights. Emmet finds it difficult to refuse – especially when Hyacinth reminds him that he said a few weeks ago how much he hated staying at hotels. He has no alternative but to accept the invitation but very soon he wishes he hadn't!

## vi Hyacinth in hospital

Hyacinth has to have a small operation carried out. Unfortunately, Richard, without telling Hyacinth, has let their private medical insurance lapse because the subscription had steadily increased and when he saw early retirement being forced upon him he knew he couldn't afford it any longer. Hyacinth therefore has to settle for a NHS public ward in their local hospital.

Once admitted she never stops complaining and causes total havoc, making life hell for her fellow patients and the staff. Onslow and Daisy visit and shatter all the illusions Hyacinth has carefully built up about her family and her important relations. Rose fancies one of the doctors.

## vii Adult education classes

The local Adult Education Centre delivers its annual broadsheet giving details of daytime courses available. With more leisure on their hands, Hyacinth sees this as an opportunity for Richard and herself to pursue a common interest (something, she says, they have never really had – apart from Sheridan). Later that morning she announces, much to Richard's horror, that she has telephoned and enrolled them both for a course called 'Tapestry and Its Appreciation'. Her reasoning being that they will be able to converse with Sheridan on an equal footing.

Much against his better judgement Richard accompanies her to the class the following evening but doesn't know where to put himself when Hyacinth causes havoc by arguing with the instructor and insisting on putting forward her views on colour and design. She has also taken three or four library books with her on the subject to which she keeps referring – plus a small example of Sheridan's handiwork which we learned earlier arrived in the post as a birthday present for Hyacinth a few days ago.

In the coffee break they run into Elizabeth who is on a first aid course, which appeals to Richard much more and then, horror of horrors, Hyacinth bumps into Onslow who is there attending a car maintenance class.

After some heated discussion at home the following morning, Hyacinth agrees to Richard's suggestion that they pull out of the Tapestry course – the instructor obviously didn't know what he was talking about anyway – and Elizabeth is called in for coffee and asked, much to her horror, if she knows whether there any vacancies on her first aid class. She plays it dumb but Hyacinth checks and she and Richard are accepted for the first aid session, where, once again, she causes a certain amount of havoc – perhaps with her bandaging which she considers looks more artistic than the normal way it is done. They learn how to give the kiss of life – which she then has to put to the test the following day on Onslow (of all people!) when he calls, skids on her polished woodblock floor and appears to be unconscious.

### viii Problems with the refuse department
A man has come in advance of the dustcart (as quite often happens) and has put all the dustbins outside the properties where – from past experience – Hyacinth knows they could sit for at least a couple of hours until the dustcart turns up. She feels that this really lets the area down and has complained several times before. Now it's happened again and just when she is expecting Councillor Mrs Nugent for morning coffee to discuss some charity work for which Hyacinth has volunteered.

After Mrs Nugent has left – and Hyacinth has been embarrassed by the presence of the dustbins – she telephones the council. Why on earth can't the dustcart pull up discreetly outside one's domicile, the dustbin be taken speedily out to the cart, quietly and tastefully emptied and the dustcart go on its way again? It doesn't seem that much to ask. Her call embarrasses Richard because the man who runs the refuse department used to be a colleague of his at the town hall.

Later, after the dustcart has finally called, Hyacinth finds that two small pieces of paper or similar rubbish have been dropped in the front garden, a small dent/nick has appeared in her bin which she swears wasn't there before, and it hasn't been put back in exactly in the right place. She again telephones the council to complain. We have a buffer scene at Daisy's and then come back to Hyacinth, half an hour later, as she goes to the dustbin to put some rubbish in it. We see her suddenly realise that the lid isn't hers – the number painted on it is Elizabeth's, next door.

Holding the lid at arm's length (and making sure no one spots her), she goes round to Liz's to ask her to swap lids – only to discover that, although Liz certainly has the wrong lid, it isn't Hyacinth's – Liz has the one belonging to the woman opposite. Hyacinth insists that Elizabeth accompanies her and, clutching their incorrect lids, they go over to see her and arrange a general swap around.

Much to Richard's horror, Hyacinth telephones the council yet again and complains in no uncertain terms about the service provided. She points out that Richard did an extremely neat and artistic job when he painted the number on their lid and asks what was the point of him going to all that trouble if the dustmen are so careless – or perhaps they get confused by numbers above ten! She asks Elizabeth round to tell her about the phone call and, whilst they are in the kitchen with Hyacinth making her the dreaded cup of coffee, she realises Richard is making a call and catches him ringing up his ex-colleague in Waste Disposal trying to take the heat out of Hyacinth's complaints. Hyacinth is furious, takes over the call and categorically states that she does not retract a single thing she said.

Unfortunately for Hyacinth, having created merry hell, she later discovers that she must have accidentally thrown a brooch away a couple of days ago. An item that is sentimental and irreplaceable (i.e. not just something that is covered by insurance). Perhaps it used to belong to her mother and Hyacinth was planning to leave it to Sheridan. As a result, she has to ring up the same official and eat humble pie as she requests a search is made. Eventually, not believing that it is impossible to make such a search (and thinking that he is just being downright awkward), she insists on going down to the refuse depot to look for it herself.

The final shot could be of Hyacinth – reasonably dressed in case someone sees her (or perhaps she changes into something more appropriate at the yard), but wearing rubber gloves as if she is doing

176

the washing up – looking down intently at the 'ground' beneath her. The camera pulls back and we discover her on the top of an enormous mountain of rubbish (Aberfan proportions), with obviously no hope whatsoever of finding anything!

## APPENDIX 2: IDEA FOR AN 'ONSLOW SPIN-OFF'

The characters of Onslow, Daisy and Rose are extremely popular with our audiences – a fact of which we have ample proof. However, their adventures on the other side of town are, of necessity, fairly limited as they tend to have a rather small 'life' beyond their own front door.

My idea would be to get them temporarily out of their own environment and put them in a situation in which I could see enormous possibilities – especially as it would also involve Elizabeth, Hyacinth's neighbour, who is also extremely popular – whilst maintaining the overall status quo for the future (i.e. the possible return of Hyacinth) if and when appropriate.

The basic idea is as follows:

We see Elizabeth locking Hyacinth's front door looking far from happy. She starts to go towards her own place then stops, returns to Hyacinth's and double checks the door before returning to Emmet. From their subsequent conversation we learn that Sheridan has decided to go to America to seek a career in dress design (or something equally precious) and that Hyacinth was so worried about him being there on his own that she has persuaded Richard that they should accompany him – at least for the first two or three months. They have left the keys of their bungalow with Elizabeth and asked her to keep an eye on the place – a task which she hates because she can well imagine just what Hyacinth's reaction would be if there was a burglary or something else went wrong in their absence.

Over on the other side of town, life continues much as usual except that on this particular morning – whilst Onslow is down at the betting shop, Daisy at the library and Rose not yet back from visiting a gentleman friend – Daddy has an unfortunate accident with the gas cooker and practically destroys the place (although, fortunately, he escapes with only minor injuries). Later in the day the official at the council is not particularly enthusiastic about the prospect of rehousing them (and certainly not immediately) because they are well behind in their rent and, of course, Onslow never makes any attempt to obtain some form of employment. 'Haven't you got a relative who can put you up until we can sort something out?' he asks.

Prompted by this, Daisy suddenly hits upon the idea of staying at Hyacinth's – a prospect which immediately appeals to Rose because of her then proximity with Emmet. They try to telephone Elizabeth but discover that she and Emmet must be out.

Later, as Elizabeth returns from the shops, she is surprised to see Onslow's old banger turn up. Whilst she is sympathetic to learn of their predicament, she is horrified when she hears Daisy's suggestion. What on earth would Hyacinth want her to do? Should she give them the keys or deny them access – either way she could still be in the wrong!

After a bit of quick thinking – and as they have nowhere to go that night – she decides that she has no alternative but to let them stay. But that one night then becomes 'just a few days' which, in turn, becomes a couple of weeks ... or so – mainly because, unbeknown to Elizabeth, Onslow has told the council that there's no rush! (In the meantime Daddy has keen admitted to an old folks nursing home but keeps trying to break out because he thinks it's a POW camp.)

The comedy would come from the way they gradually take over Hyacinth's home and start to live there in much the same way as they did in their own place and with additional comedic possibilities. For instance, I can see Onslow not liking Hyacinth's TV because it doesn't respond to being thumped (he also doesn't understand their remote control) and Daisy trying to make her usual romantic over-tures to Onslow and the latter – as well as his normal lack of interest – being totally turned off by the fact that they are in Hyacinth's bed!

Rose could be seen flirting with Emmet, who, much to Elizabeth's horror, is beginning to show interest. Emmet could then start to come up with his own excuses to go round to Hyacinth (ostensibly to check things out for Liz but, in reality, to pursue his own interests!).

After a few days Onslow would have the old car from their garden shifted over there – because the dog just isn't happy sleeping on Hyacinth's sofa – and, of course, the neighbours begin to think that squatters have moved in.

As Elizabeth sees all this happening, she could become even more of a nervous wreck when asked in for a 'mug of cocoa' than she was when having coffee with Hyacinth. She would become more and more manic about whether she had done the right thing – her end of telephone calls from Hyacinth would become a running gag as we realise that she is getting herself into deeper and deeper water. She could invent umpteen different excuses to go round there to check on the latest situation, whilst, at the same time, Emmet is telling her not to worry about it.

On the postman's first visit after Onslow has re-sited the old car, he would be shaken up by the dog almost as much as if it had been Hyacinth!

Various 'upmarket' local characters would call and be amazed to find the new occupants. Daisy and Onslow could avail themselves of a civic invitation sent to Hyacinth (attending as Hyacinth and Richard's 'representatives' – much to the horror of the hosts, etc.). Daisy could start to borrow some of Hyacinth's clothes.

There are also great possibilities with the use of the apartment purchased by Hyacinth and Richard (in the fourth series) in the huge country mansion. Onslow et al. could find the keys to this flat in a drawer at the bungalow and decide that they might as well give themselves a break in the country. There could be a lot of fun from their arrival (to the horror of other residents) and presence at the upmarket mansion and their feeble attempt to temporarily mix with the country set in the hope that, as Hyacinth's relatives, they might be shown some hospitality.

There is also the fact that the apartment is unbelievably tiny – or 'bijou' as Hyacinth preferred to call it. The ceilings all slope and, overall, there is very little space. The only time they paid Hyacinth a visit there Onslow and Daisy got stuck trying to pass each other in the kitchen! To have them arrive with plans to stay a few days – having temporarily forgotten about the lack of space – could present some wonderful comedic opportunities.

Overall there are a lot of possibilities.

# APPENDIX 3: IDEA FOR A SPECIAL

After the titles we see the exterior of Hyacinth's and, on going in closer, hear the sound of hoovering. Inside we find Elizabeth working away like a mad thing – an array of cleaning materials in evidence.

The doorbell rings and Elizabeth cautiously opens the front door to reveal Emmet. She lets him in and immediately goes back to her cleaning whilst he asks her how much longer she is going to be – she's already been there two hours! They had agreed they were going into town to a sale that was on – at this rate there will be nothing left. From their conversation we learn that Hyacinth and Richard have been in America for the past month. This had come about because Sheridan had left college and decided to go into the world of dress design and had taken up a training opportunity in New York. Hyacinth was so concerned for his safety that she had insisted that Richard and herself go over there to see that he wasn't getting into the wrong company.

They had left their keys with Elizabeth. Their absence has delighted Emmet who has felt 'free' for a whole month. The fact that Hyacinth is due to return this afternoon is affecting his morale very badly. He cannot understand why Elizabeth is doing all this cleaning – Hyacinth left them the keys in the event of an emergency not so she could become a char lady. Elizabeth admits this but goes on to say how Hyacinth would react if she came back and found evidence of dust! She says she's nearly finished and they agree that they will leave for the sale at 11.30. Emmet goes and Elizabeth continues her cleaning.

On the other side of town Onslow enters the sitting room and starts to watch TV. Usual recognisable day-to-day life in that household.

Back on the 'superior' side of town we see Emmet reading a newspaper. He stops and looks at the clock. Although it registers 11.40 there is no sign of Elizabeth returning from Hyacinth's. He is then horrified to see a taxi pull up next door and Hyacinth start to emerge – they've obviously caught an earlier flight. Her presence back in the area immediately starts to affect him. He appears quite groggy.

Elizabeth has just finished her cleaning and is checking the kitchen. She hears keys in the front door and, understandably, wonders who it is. She then hears Hyacinth remark to Richard saying that Elizabeth

180

has obviously been in and foolishly forgotten to reset the burglar alarm. We see Elizabeth's reaction to this and she starts to go into the hall. In the meantime, Hyacinth has swept back outside again to organise the unloading of their luggage.

Emmet notes this and realises that Hyacinth can't have met up with Elizabeth and wonders how to warn the latter. He dashes to the phone. Elizabeth is hovering in the lounge waiting for Hyacinth to come back. The phone rings and, having hesitated a moment or two, she decides that she had better answer it. As she does so, Hyacinth sweeps round the corner and beats her to it, much to Emmet's horror who immediately pretends to be selling double glazing! Hyacinth turns his offer down. She says hello to Elizabeth, who makes her excuse for being at Hyacinth's the fact she has popped in to water her houseplants.

Hyacinth immediately goes into the lounge to check that Elizabeth has given them just the right amount – it's almost correct! Richard appears at the lounge door and says how nice it is to be home at which point Hyacinth comments how lucky they are to have quality furniture that, even after a month, doesn't show the dust. Elizabeth makes her excuses and departs with Hyacinth's invitation for her and Emmet to come round for coffee and hear all about their adventures in the States.

Another scene at Onslow's and then back to Hyacinth's where she is busy organising the sorting out of the contents of their luggage – nine suitcases. Richard goes into the kitchen and calls back to Hyacinth, commenting on the amount of mail piled up on the worktop. Hyacinth joins him and is appalled that such a huge number of letters could have been left in one pile. Surely Elizabeth could have separated them into various categories – first class, second class, bills, junk mail, etc.

Next door, Elizabeth is trying to assure Emmet that having Hyacinth back need not be as bad as he thinks. Perhaps she's changed a little in the last month – although we realise that she thinks this is pretty unlikely. In the mail Hyacinth finds a letter from the publishers of a new travel magazine which she started to buy a few months ago. We learn that before she went to America the magazine had run a competition in conjunction with the launch of a new brand of exclusive luggage. The competition involved coming up with the best advertising slogan for the new luggage and the prize was a trip to Paris for four people on the Orient Express, seven days in an internationally renowned hotel, return air trip by Concorde, plus ten items of the new luggage. According to the letter Hyacinth has won!

She is naturally ecstatic. Richard asks when the trip will be and is somewhat put out to learn that it is in six days' time. The letter asks Hyacinth to contact the magazine as soon as possible and she is worried that their being away might mean that they have lost the prize. Richard wryly comments that presumably Hyacinth will alert the local paper etc. of her win, which, of course, is precisely what she has in mind.

However, in the middle of outlining her 'publicity plans' she suddenly goes strangely quiet. When Richard asks why, she reluctantly reveals that she has just spotted a mention of the prize winning slogan at the end of the letter – and it isn't hers! It's obviously a typical computer error – someone else's slogan has won but Hyacinth's name and address has been put on the letter.

Richard is all for her ringing up the magazine and owning up but she says that she needs time to think. She rationalises that whoever was the real winner might not be the right sort of person to do the prize justice and she could well be doing the magazine a favour by being the class of person who will be quite at home with the luxury on offer. She tells Richard that only the two of them know about the error and that it is a wonderful opportunity. We learn that, despite all her claims to have travelled the world, apart from their trip on the *QE2* and their visit to New York they have only been to Bridlington and Eastbourne. She'd certainly love to go to Paris.

Although it is against Richard's better judgement he reluctantly agrees to them going. She rings up the magazine and apologises for the delay in responding but she's been 'heavily tied up with charitable work' and is told that the prize is still available to them. She puts the telephone down elated. She starts to think who they are going to invite to go with them to make up the four. Richard suggests Daisy and Onslow, which doesn't go down at all well.

Another scene at Onslow and Daisy's where, coincidentally, they are discussing whether they can afford two nights B&B at Morecombe.

Then back to Hyacinth's where she is pacing up and down the

lounge whilst considering who the other two could be. She says that she needs two friends – which prompts Richard to comment that finding them isn't going to be easy! Hyacinth then glances out of the window and sees Elizabeth and Emmet returning from the sale. Of course, the obvious solution – especially as whenever she meets Emmet he looks as if he could do with a rest.

Hyacinth rushes outside and intercepts them. She insists that they come in saying that she is going to tell them something which will definitely be to their advantage. Emmet is, as usual, extremely reluctant but, hoping it may be news that they are moving, agrees. He is delighted to learn that Hyacinth is going away again and comments how lovely her trip sounds and how jealous he is. It is only at this point that Hyacinth reveals her plans to include them. Whilst Elizabeth certainly has her reservations about spending ten days with Hyacinth, she is obviously excited about the prospect of such a trip. Emmet's doubts are far greater than his sister's!

Using the excuse that they need to look into Emmet's work plans (music lessons and rehearsals), they return next door. They are very surprised when Hyacinth runs after them saying that it is part of the competition's rules that they must keep the fact that she has won strictly to themselves. Back home Elizabeth and Emmet almost fall out over the pros and cons of the trip. Eventually, after Elizabeth has pointed out that they don't have to spend all the time in Paris with Hyacinth, he agrees that they will go. Elizabeth phones Hyacinth with their decision.

Various scenes over the next few days with the plans getting tighter, Emmet getting more worried, Elizabeth getting excited but apprehensive. Hyacinth is in her seventh heaven – she appears to have obtained every Paris guidebook on the market and is making copious notes. She has decided to tell Daisy and Onslow only at the last minute and then, in order to avoid questions about the competition and the winning slogan, she plans to say that it is all connected with an offer made to Richard by one of the larger Railtrack companies who are planning to expand into the Continent and are looking for an administration manager.

Two days before they are due to depart the tickets arrive, plus the details of their very high-class accommodation in Paris. Also the other part of the prize – a set of twelve different type and sized suitcases. As they already have ten, Richard is fed up to find suitcases everywhere he turns.

On the big day we see them leave by limousine provided as part of the prize. As the numerous items of their new luggage are loaded along with Elizabeth and Emmet's two suitcases, Hyacinth tries to ensure the whole thing is kept very low profile – in total contrast to what would have keen her normal attitude in these circumstances. Emmet is delighted. Perhaps she *is* a changed woman – but later he realises he is wrong.

We see them board the English side of the train in London, arrive at Folkestone and transfer on to the ferry where, of course, they are in the special section reserved for Orient Express passengers. Hyacinth suddenly remembers that Paris is the renowned centre of the fashion world and, in view of Sheridan's career in dress design, this gives her an idea. Paris is obviously much 'safer' than New York – plus the fact that Sheridan would also be so much closer to Mummy. She declares that she is going to keep an eye open and take a note of all the haute-couture houses that could benefit from Sheridan's talent.

Back in the UK, Onslow, Daisy and Rose have a major problem. We find them waiting at the council offices and learn that, whilst the three of them were out, Daddy had an unfortunate accident with the gas cooker and practically destroyed the place – although, fortunately, he escaped with only minor injuries. It does, however, mean he has to stay in hospital for a couple of days.

On board the ferry Hyacinth deliberately leaves and returns to the Orient Express section several times in order that other 'ordinary' passengers will be in no doubt that she is travelling in style. She then suddenly becomes worried that the hotel might not be expecting them -- all sorts of doubts keep going through her mind and she keeps dragging Richard away from the others to have private discussions.

At the council offices the man in the housing department is not very enthusiastic about the prospect of rehousing Onslow and Daisy immediately (especially, of course, as Onslow never attempts to obtain any form of employment). 'Haven't you a relative who can put you up for a few days until we can sort something out?', he asks.

Prompted by this Daisy suddenly hits upon the idea of them temporarily staying at Hyacinth's – after all, they're away in France for a week. They try to telephone Elizabeth, knowing that she still has Hyacinth's keys from when she was in the States, but there's obviously no reply.

We come back to see Hyacinth lording it up having dinner on the French side of the Orient Express. She is obviously totally in her element as she snaps her fingers at the stewards and generally makes sure everybody knows she is there and familiar with the set-up whilst, at the same time, quietly instructing Richard not to mention that this is their first trip.

As the day is wearing on, Onslow decides that they had better go over to Hyacinth's. We see them call at Elizabeth's but, gaining no reply, Onslow decides he has no alternative but to break in through Hyacinth's kitchen door. He succeeds because, in the rush of leaving, Richard has forgotten to set the burglar alarm.

In Paris, Hyacinth et al. arrive at the wonderful hotel – again by limousine. Hyacinth's attempts to speak French are appalling and she is very put out to discover that both Elizabeth and Emmet are reasonably fluent. The only advantage seems to be that the French are inclined to pronounce Bucket as 'Bouquet', which obviously pleases her enormously. Hyacinth and Richard have a suite and Elizabeth and Emmet are given a superior-grade bedroom.

Whilst she and Richard are unpacking, Hyacinth suddenly becomes worried about Elizabeth and Emmet – as brother and sister – sharing a room. She discusses it with Richard who volunteers to share with Emmet. Hyacinth doesn't like the sound of this arrangement any better but is determined to check out whether Elizabeth has a double- or twin-bedded room. She is appalled to find it is a double and asks Richard to talk to reception but then hastily changes her mind because of the circumstances of their visit.

Various adventures in Paris starting the following day could include the following:

1) Hyacinth is determined to join in with the French way of life. She sits with the others outside a typical Parisian pâtisserie and orders coffee and a *pain au chocolat* warm. Then she takes her first bite into this (made especially for the filming) and a huge burst of hot chocolate shoots out and goes all down the front of her smart outfit – much to the others' huge but disguised amusement.

2) Hyacinth makes a big thing about wanting to go up the Eiffel Tower only to discover, once at the top, that she has no head for heights. She has to be given smelling salts by the first-aid people and escorted into the lift by security staff.

3) Emmet decides to brighten Richard's life by taking him to the Moulin Rouge (or similar). Richard has his doubts but agrees to go along with the idea. They concoct a suitable excuse (perhaps to do with supposedly visiting a late-night art show at the Pompidou Centre – a venue they know Hyacinth doesn't want to visit because of its 'ultra-modern' feel). We wouldn't go with them but there could be a near thing, later, when Hyacinth questions Richard about the art he saw ('there weren't any nudes, were there?') and when she almost sees a ticket for the 'naughty' show amongst the items Richard takes out of his pockets before retiring for the night.

We can also cash in on the established fact that Elizabeth is always in fear of Hyacinth and that Emmet can't stand her, which gives us instantly recognisable 'relationship' scenarios between Hyacinth and these two that could arise during the trip.

For instance, as they pass the Paris Opera, Hyacinth could drag Emmet inside, insisting that they would both benefit by watching rehearsals. Once in the foyer she would embarrass him even further when she bursts into her feeble attempt at some well-known aria.

She could tell Elizabeth that whilst in Paris they must go and try on some clothes at Yves St Laurent. On arriving (Elizabeth extremely reluctantly), Hyacinth is told that an appointment is necessary (which is the case) and she then embarrasses Elizabeth even further by taking her usual defensive stance of 'surely not in my case?'

Hyacinth could lose Richard's wallet by accidentally dropping it over the side of the *bateau-mouche* and then causes a huge furore by insisting that the boat goes back and that divers are called in.

A buffer scene at Hyacinth's where Onslow and the others are settling in. Daisy is serving up smoked salmon taken from Hyacinth's freezer.

Back in Paris, it is their second day. We establish that Hyacinth never trusts Richard to look after their passports when they are on a trip, and she therefore keeps hers and his together in a special leather pouch. He now needs his to buy some more French francs and

Hyacinth is horrified to discover that she can't find their passports. She and Richard search all their empty suitcases but with no success. They go to reception to see if they've been handed in and they haven't. They are advised to contact the local police and the British Embassy.

However, in the meantime, the hotel says they are prepared to give them the French currency they require but, in order to satisfy their own security regulations, Hyacinth and Richard will need to have their photographs taken in their ID room. They agree to what seems a reasonable request (fun of Hyacinth wanting to check her make-up and hair and telling them which is her 'best side'), but when they are out later, Hyacinth suddenly starts to worry that maybe the real reason the photographs were taken was because the hotel suspects that they are there under false pretences. Perhaps they suspect a 'story' and the pictures are being circulated to the Paris press! From then on she drags Richard into doorways etc. whenever they see a *gendarme* or a police car and keeps an eagle eye out for the paparazzi.

In the afternoon they all go off to Montmartre where, against Hyacinth's advice, Elizabeth agrees to have her portrait sketched by one of the many pavement artists. Hyacinth is appalled and drags Richard away, saying that they will be back shortly. How could Elizabeth lower her self-esteem by letting some amateur Renoir draw her picture? However, when they return a few minutes later the end result is a very charming likeness which brings out all her friend's best features and Hyacinth immediately becomes very jealous that Elizabeth has been drawn and she hasn't. She admits that she was wrong and Richard pays for her to have her portrait done. Elizabeth and Emmet wander off to look in a shop and return just as the artist is finishing. The end result makes Hyacinth look horrendous – an ageing battleaxe. Hyacinth is furious and pushes the artist's easel over as she storms off. A highly embarrassed Richard hands over a wad of French francs by way of an apology.

That night they decide to have dinner out rather than in the hotel. Hyacinth dresses up to the nines and off they go.

Meanwhile, Onslow, Daisy, Rose and the dog are really making themselves at home – after only forty-eight hours the place is already beginning to look 'lived in'. Onslow doesn't like their telly because it doesn't go on when he thumps it – he actually has to use the remote control.

Back at the Paris hotel, around midnight, we see a taxi pull up and the four of them scramble out having had an enjoyable evening. Emmet and Richard are very slightly the worse for wear. Hyacinth and the others go to reception and ask for their room keys only to be told that they don't have their rooms any longer, in fact they've been re-let! They are told that their belongings have been removed and put in the baggage store.

Hyacinth demands to know what is going on and asks to see the night manager. He tells them that the hotel received two faxes a couple of hours ago – one specifically for the hotel and one addressed to Hyacinth. They were both from a magazine publisher in England. The fax to the hotel told them that Mrs Bucket is in France under false pretences and that they are not eligible to stay at the hotel. The magazine would pay the bill up to this point but no further. Hyacinth is horrified – not only that things have turned out like this but that Elizabeth and Emmet are privy to it all.

The fax to Hyacinth says that, although there had, admittedly, been an error on the part of the magazine, Hyacinth must have obviously realised this as soon as she saw that the slogan in their original letter wasn't hers and she should have admitted this. They took a very dim view of this sort of behaviour and were acting accordingly. A room had been booked for them elsewhere for that night and tickets arranged on the ferry tomorrow, but that is the limit of the magazine's goodwill.

Hyacinth is distraught and hugely embarrassed. They ask for their luggage back and are taken to the baggage store. Elizabeth and Emmet's belongings have all been repacked in their two suitcases and are brought out first. They are followed by four large black plastic bin liners, which are handed over to Hyacinth and Richard. The manager explains that the magazine has asked them to confiscate their suitcases because they are part of the prize they hadn't officially won. (Their passports would also be returned to them having been discovered by a chambermaid behind a bedside cabinet.)

A taxi is called and they walk back through the elegant reception area where the sight of Hyacinth and Richard carrying (dragging) the

bin liners causes quite a stir among the various high-class residents
returning from casinos, night clubs, etc. especially with Hyacinth in
her finery. The manager accompanies them to the taxi and gives the
driver an address. We mix to see the taxi pulling up outside a terribly
squalid hotel in an extremely seedy area. Hyacinth is appalled, especially
when she sees the actual room. Even more so when she learns that
all four of them have to sleep there. She gets Emmet to ask the
woman in charge if there is another hotel in the area but they are
told that there is unlikely to be any vacancies at this time of night.

We mix to see Daisy and Onslow in Hyacinth and Richard's bed.
Daisy, of course, finds the rather smarter atmosphere 'romantic', but
Onslow is totally turned off by the thought of being in Hyacinth's
bed.

Back in the squalid hotel, Richard is telling Hyacinth that it is
only fair that Elizabeth and Emmet have the bed – after all, they're
the innocent parties in all this. After some hurried discussion, she
reluctantly agrees and she and Richard bed down on the floor using
two bin liners as pillows – the other two having been used by Hyacinth
to form a barrier between Elizabeth and Emmet in the bed. Quite a
come down from a five-star hotel!

The next day we see Onslow, Daisy and Rose saying how much
they like their new lifestyle and they discuss the fact that they still
have another five days before Hyacinth returns. Onslow rings the
man at the council to tell him that they won't need a place for a
few days. Daisy is running out of things to wear and raids Hyacinth's
wardrobe. We see Hyacinth, Richard, Elizabeth and Emmet get off
the train at Boulogne and struggle on to the ferry. We establish that
they *would* have purchased some cheap suitcases but, when Richard
lost his wallet, this also included his credit cards. Unfortunately,
Elizabeth doesn't have a credit card and Emmet has reached the limit
on his. This means that Hyacinth and Richard still have their belongings
in the bin liners, which causes a reasonable degree of suspicion at
Customs and everything is searched.

Once on board, Hyacinth can't face the indignity of being seen in
the ship's lounges with bin liners so decides to stay on deck with
them where, of course, she looks like some overdressed bag lady.

We see a taxi turn up outside Hyacinth's. She and the other three emerge and, dragging their bin liners, Hyacinth and Richard let themselves into the bungalow. The final straw comes when they find Onslow et al. are in residence!

## APPENDIX 4: IDEA FOR A MILLENNIUM EPISODE

Bearing in mind that Hyacinth's life has always revolved around holding functions (candlelight suppers etc.), it is obvious that she would see the Millennium as an excuse for laying on a really special 'do' – and going out of her way to ensure that it is far more mind-boggling and glitzy than anyone else's.

She would enthusiastically discuss her plans with a very bored Richard and show him the dome-shaped canapés she has been experimenting with – but would then be horrified to discover from the local paper, conversations with Elizabeth and from various telephone calls that other people are planning exactly the same sort of things.

Being Hyacinth, she is determined not to be beaten on any aspect of her function and comes up with even more outrageous ideas including writing to well-known people asking them if they would like to attend. A few days later the postman turns up with a huge sackful of mail which Hyacinth, of course, assumes are all acceptances. The reverse is the case.

During the course of all this she decides that in order to mark the Millennium, they should make Sheridan a particularly large monetary gift, which, naturally, doesn't go down at all well with Richard.

On the other side of town Daisy is trying to persuade Onslow that the Millennium calls for a complete overhaul of their marriage and way of life. Hyacinth then decides that perhaps she was originally aiming a bit too high and decides to try and organise a street party. She gets Richard to put notices through the letter boxes of everyone in the road to see if anyone is interested. Only a few hours later they are all returned marked 'Sorry, not interested'.

Hyacinth then decides to go completely the other way again and, much to Richard's horror, her plans for a special 'do' get bigger and bigger as she becomes even more determined that she will have better food and drink than anyone else in the neighbourhood – her conception of 'neighbourhood' being a radius of at least fifty miles. Eventually, she comes up with the idea of holding the function somewhere 'historical'. She decides that she is going to talk to Lord Lichfield (whom they met on the *QE2*) and see whether he would be interested in holding a 'joint' function with her at Shugborough. (We would probably be able to film a meeting there with him as he was very helpful – and delightful company – when we were with him before.)

Needless to say, he would find a good reason for declining but she would accept this because 'obviously he just couldn't face coping with the huge number of my guests who would want to attend'.

During all this Hyacinth would regularly tell Elizabeth her ever-changing plans and make her swear on oath to keep them secret. In reality, the latter would rush home to Emmet and they would collapse in hopeless laughter discussing Hyacinth's latest ludicrous idea. Emmet, of course, is also busy trying to work out how they are going to get out of attending whatever function Hyacinth eventually holds.

In the end, Hyacinth decides to hire a marquee ('after all the Queen uses one for her functions at Buck. House') and gets Richard to use his connection with the local council to gain permission to have it erected in the park. This he manages to do, with them only giving permission on the strict understanding that no one from the council will receive an invite.

Come the big night everything is laid out beautifully in the marquee and Hyacinth is convinced that the various people she has invited will turn up, and the only reason she hasn't heard back from that many of them is because their responses have obviously somehow gone astray in the post. 'What, two hundred of them!' says Richard. Those people who have replied have all either come up with an excuse for not being able to attend or have said that they will make it if they possibly can. Hyacinth sees this as their way of saying that if they can't find anything better they will be there. As she knows there won't be anything better, she is still convinced that there will be a large number of guests.

As the evening draws on, only Elizabeth and Emmet arrive much to Hyacinth's embarrassment. Shortly after eleven o'clock Hyacinth looks outside to see if there is any sign of guests approaching and happens to spot a tramp lying on a bench. She comes back inside the marquee and, without referring to what she has just seen, announces to the other three – who are bored stiff and extremely cold – that she has suddenly had a brilliant idea. She says that she now realises that for far too long she has seen herself too high up the social ladder. 'In the final analysis we're all human beings, no one more important than anyone else.' She decides there and then that the Millennium is the ideal time to make amends for this and instructs Richard and Emmet to round up all the vagrants they can find in the park and bring them in. As they reluctantly go outside to comply with this request, Hyacinth tells Elizabeth that, in future, she is going to strive to be much more humble. At the same time she asks her to use Emmet's mobile phone to try and ring the local paper and contact the regional TV station!

There would then be a time lapse of half an hour or so by which time a dozen or so down-and-outs are arriving. Hyacinth dishes out plates and invites them to help themselves. They can't believe their luck (a couple of them kiss Hyacinth in their gratitude – which she is not too happy about) as they start to load their plates up.

Richard then announces that there is only fifteen minutes to go before midnight, which prompts Hyacinth to burst into song. After only thirty seconds of this the vagrants look at each other and hastily depart – some even leaving their plates of food behind. Hyacinth is in despair. She reluctantly decides to ring Onslow and Daisy to wish them a happy Millennium. Richard then looks highly embarrassed and says he knows they won't be in because, having been the guests of honour on that trip on the *QE2* and met up with Lord Lichfield, Onslow and Daisy received an invitation to his Millennium function at Shugborough. Hyacinth just can't believe it.

## APPENDIX 5: COMPLETE LIST OF EPISODES (WITH ORIGINAL TRANSMISSION DATES)

### Series 1

**Ep. 1** Initial 'pilot' episode. Problems with Daddy. 29.10.90 (pp. 15–24)
**Ep. 2** Hyacinth asks new vicar to tea. 05.11.90 (pp. 24–25)

**Ep. 3** Hyacinth visits her favourite stately home. 12.11.90 (pp. 25–26)
**Ep. 4** Hyacinth has problems with a charity shop and Rose's love life – to say nothing of Daddy's! 19.11.90 (pp. 27–28)
**Ep. 5** Hyacinth's social standing at a church function is jeopardised when Daisy wants Onslow to be more romantic. 26.11.90 (pp. 28–30)
**Ep. 6** Hyacinth could never have envisaged how this family christening would turn out. 03.12.90 (pp. 30–34)


## Series 2

**Ep. 1** Hyacinth is very suspicious of a man who seems to have moved in next door with Liz – it's her brother. 01.9.91 (pp. 36–37)
**Ep. 2** Hyacinth is delighted to provide Richard as chauffeur to the eminent Mrs Fortescue … until they meet Daisy. 08.09.91 (pp. 39–41)
**Ep. 3** Hyacinth's candlelight supper is upset by Rose's boyfriends. She sings loudly to drown out the argument. 15.09.91 (pp. 41–42)
**Ep. 4** Hyacinth and Richard go for a golfing weekend and the Major tries to get romantic with her. 22.09.01 (pp. 42–44)
**Ep. 5** Daisy and Onslow lose Daddy. Having found him in register office they then have other problems at Violet's, whose husband, Bruce, is up a tree! 29.09.91 (p. 44)
**Ep. 6** Hyacinth reluctantly accepts an invitation to Onslow's birthday lunch and organises her own pre-lunch drinks session. She is pleased that they are being picked up by Rose's boyfriend's limo – except that it turns out to be a hearse! 06.10.91 (pp. 44–46)
**Ep. 7** Richard hears he has to take early retirement which, as far as Hyacinth is concerned, is not as important as trying to rehearse with poor Emmet at the church hall. 13.10.91 (pp. 46–47)
**Ep. 8** Daddy causes chaos in the children's department of a local store – and Mrs Nugent is almost privy to it. 20.10.91 (pp. 47–48)
**Ep. 9** Hyacinth is extremely excited about the arrival of her new three-piece suite – especially as the delivery van will have the royal coat of arms on the side! 27.10.91 (pp. 48–49)
**Ep. 10** Hyacinth organises a picnic in the country for Daddy. Unfortunately when they go to pick him up he pinches their car and a chase ensues using Onslow's old banger. 03.11.91 (pp. 49–50)

**Christmas Special 1991** Hyacinth decides that Richard, dressed as Santa Claus, should help dispense presents to the old folk at the church hall. 25.12.92 (pp. 60–62)


Series 3


**Ep. 1** Hyacinth is delighted at the prospect of spending more time with Richard now he's retired whereas Richard is not so keen. A man leaves a large dog on her drive. 06.09.92 (pp. 65–67)
**Ep. 2** Hyacinth's plans to help Richard make the most of his retirement have to be put aside because of Rose's behaviour. 13.09.92 (pp. 67–68)
**Ep. 3** Hyacinth and Richard take over Violet's country cottage for a couple of days and events take several unexpected turns. 30.09.92 (p. 68)
**Ep. 4** In order to keep up with someone's elaborate holiday plans, Hyacinth makes enquiries about very expensive holidays before becoming involved in church cleaning duties. 27.09.92 (pp. 68–70)
**Ep. 5** Hyacinth provides Richard with a hobby in the form of a video camera. However, it rather backfires on her. 04.10.92 (pp. 70–71)
**Ep. 6** Hyacinth's desire to be seen as interested in art coincides with Daddy's desire to join the Foreign Legion. 11.10.92 (pp. 71–72)
**Ep. 7** Hyacinth's plans for a nautical supper take an unexpected turn – as does the boat! 18.10.92 (pp. 72–73)


Series 4


**Ep. 1** Hyacinth concocts an elaborate plan on the golf course in order for Richard to impress a potential employer. 05.09.93 (pp. 84–86)
**Ep. 2** Hyacinth's plans to buy a small weekend retreat in the country go somewhat awry. 12.09.93 (pp. 86–87)
**Ep. 3** Hyacinth invents the outdoor–indoors luxury barbecue. 19.09.93 (pp. 87–88)
**Ep. 4** Hyacinth volunteers to meet the Ladies' Luncheon Club special guest at the railway station – but it all goes horribly wrong. 26.09.93 (pp. 88–90)

**Ep. 5** Hyacinth is still seeking her country retreat. She thinks she has succeeded. 03.10.93 (pp. 90–94)

**Ep. 6** Hyacinth and Richard move into what is really a tiny flat in the roof area of a large mansion. She calls it 'olde worlde bijou' – Richard finds it anything but that. 10.10.93 (pp. 94–97)

**Ep. 7** Hyacinth volunteers Richard's services to mend the church hall electrics – with interesting consequences. 17.10.93 (pp. 97–100)

**Christmas Special 1993** Hyacinth and Richard embark on a cruise on the *QE2* only to discover that Onslow and Daisy are guests of honour on the same cruise, having won a competition. 25.12.93 (pp. 100–115)

(No new series in 1994 because of the non-availability of Patricia Routledge. However, we did make a 'special' for Christmas.)

**Christmas Special 1994** Richard goes down with a fungal infection in his foot, which Hyacinth insists he maintains is gout as this is classier. She is also very anxious to re-equip her kitchen with a certain type of worktop. 26.12.94 (pp. 119–124)

## Series 5

**Ep. 1** Much to the Vicar's horror Hyacinth volunteers to help look after the old folk on a day's outing to the seaside – which includes a funfair! 03.09.95 (pp. 129–131)

**Ep. 2** Hyacinth is mortified not to receive an invitation to the Mayor's fancy dress ball and demands that Richard rectifies this oversight. Later she wishes he hadn't. 10.09.95 (pp. 131–134)

**Ep. 3** Richard forgets their wedding anniversary but manages to get away with it by telling Hyacinth that he has arranged for their home to be fitted with a burglar alarm as a surprise. 17.09.95 (p. 134)

**Ep. 4** Hyacinth plans a riverside supper with 'riparian entertainment' but her plans go badly wrong. 24.09.95 (pp. 134–136)

**Ep. 5** It is Richard's birthday and in order to keep up with some neighbours she buys him some skis. 01.10.95 (pp. 137–140)

**Ep. 6** Hyacinth and Richard attend an auction at a stately home. The wine she buys goes straight to Hyacinth's head. 08.10.95 (pp. 140–141)

**Ep. 7** Hyacinth hears that Emmet is planning a production of *The Boy Friend* and is keen to be involved. However, sorting out Daddy's insistence in taking over Onslow's house has to take priority. 15.10.95 (pp. 141–143)

**Ep. 8** Still keen to be part of *The Boy Friend*, Hyacinth goes down to the church hall and terrifies all concerned. She then insists that the Vicar, Emmet and Liz attend the barbecue she is holding in Violet's garden. 22.10.95 (pp. 143–145)

**Ep. 9** Mortified that she only came second at a craft fair, Hyacinth 'borrows' a Rolls-Royce from a showroom in order to impress the lady who won. However, it's not quite that simple. 29.10.95 (pp. 145–148)

**Ep. 10** Hyacinth advertises her services as a social host but this term is misconstrued by the people who respond. 05.11.95 (pp. 148–151)

**Christmas Special 1995** Hyacinth tries to take over the organisation of a pageant at the church hall but, surprisingly, on hearing that she will be in charge, no one volunteers to be involved. 26.12.95 (pp. 153–159)

## APPENDIX 6: MEMBERS OF THE CAST

### Regular cast members

| | |
|---|---|
| Hyacinth | *Patricia Routledge* |
| Richard | *Clive Swift* |
| Daisy | *Judy Cornwell* |
| Onslow | *Geoffrey Hughes* |
| Rose | *Mary Millar* (Series 1 only); *Shirley Stelfox* |
| Elizabeth | *Josephine Tewson* |
| Emmet | *David Griffin* |

### Semi-regular members

| | |
|---|---|
| Vicar | *Jeremy Gittins* |
| His Wife | *Marion Barron* |
| The Postman | *David Janson* |
| The Milkman | *Robert Rawles* |
| Violet | *Anna Dawson* |
| Daddy | *George Webb* |